The Conflict Between

EQUILIBRIUM

and

DISEQUILIBRIUM THEORIES

The Case of
the U.S. Labor Market

Richard E. Quandt
Harvey S. Rosen

1988

W. E. UPJOHN INSTITUTE for Employment Research

Library of Congress Cataloging-in-Publication Data

Quandt, Richard E.
    The conflict between equilibrium and disequilibrium theories : the
case of the U.S. labor market / Richard E. Quandt, Harvey S. Rosen.
        p.   cm.
    Bibliography: p.
    Includes index.
    ISBN 0-88099-061-9.   ISBN 0-88099-060-0 (pbk.)
    1. Labor supply—United States—Econometric models.
2. Equilibrium (Economics)—Mathematical models.   3. Unemployment—
United States—Econometric models.   4. Manpower Policy—United
States—Econometric models.   I. Rosen, Harvey S.   II. W.E. Upjohn
Institute for Employment Research.   III. Title.
  HD5724.Q36 1988
  331.12'0973—dc19   88-10618
                                                                        CIP

Copyright © 1988
by the
W. E. UPJOHN INSTITUTE
FOR EMPLOYMENT RESEARCH

300 South Westnedge Ave.
Kalamazoo, Michigan 49007

THE INSTITUTE, a nonprofit research organization, was established on July
1, 1945. It is an activity of the W. E. Upjohn Unemployment Trustee Corpora-
tion, which was formed in 1932 to administer a fund set aside by the late
Dr. W. E. Upjohn for the purpose of carrying on "research into the causes
and effects of unemployment and measures for the alleviation of unemployment."

The facts presented in this study and the observations and viewpoints expressed are the sole responsibility of the authors. They do not necessarily represent
positions of the W. E. Upjohn Institute for Employment Research.

ii

Authors

Richard E. Quandt received his A.B. dgree from Princeton University in 1952 and his Ph.D. in Economics from Harvard University in 1957. He became an assistant professor at Princeton University in 1956 and a professor in 1964. He served as chairman of the Economics Department from 1968-71 and 1985-88. He is a fellow of the Econometric Society and of the American Statistical Association.

Harvey S. Rosen received his A.B. degree from the University of Michigan in 1970 and his Ph.D. in Economics from Harvard University in 1974. He joined the faculty of Princeton University as an assistant professor in that year, and became a professor in 1984. In addition to his position at Princeton, Rosen is a research associate of the National Bureau of Economic Research, a fellow of the Econometric Society, and coeditor of the *Papers and Proceedings of the American Economic Association.*

Acknowledgements

We are grateful to the Upjohn Institute for financial support, to Stephen Woodbury for useful suggestions, and to Elvira Krespach for superb assistance with the computations.

Contents

1 Introduction 1
    1.1 The Policy Issues 1
    1.2 The Methodological Issues 2
    1.3 Goals of this Monograph 5
    Notes 6

2 Equilibrium vs. Disequilibrium Labor Market Analysis 7
    2.1 Equilibrium Labor Market Analysis 7
    2.2 Disequilibrium Labor Market Analysis 9
    Notes 15

3 Formulating a Disequilibrium Model 17
    3.1 Introductory Remarks 17
    3.2 The Disequilibrium Model 19
    3.3 Econometric Issues 25
    Appendix 3.1 The Role of the Jacobian of the Transformation 36
    Appendix 3.2 Derivations of the Disequilibrium
                       Likelihood Function 38
    Notes 42

4 Estimating the Disequilibrium Model 43
    4.1 Restatement of the Model 43
    4.2 Data 44
    4.3 Stochastic Specification and Estimation Procedure 44
    4.4 Parameter Estimates 45
    4.5 Discussion of Results 47
    4.6 Summary 59
    Appendix 4.1 Data 60
    Appendix 4.2 Dynamics in the Disequilibrium Model 62
    Appendix 4.3 Computation of the Natural Rate of Unemployment .63
    Notes 64

5 The Equilibrium Model 67
    5.1 The Basic Structure 67
    5.2 Modeling Expectations 71
    5.3 Parameter Estimates 76
    5.4 Other Results for the Rational Expectations Model 80

5.5 Evaluating the Equilibrium Models 83
Appendix 5.1 Dynamics in the Equilibrium Model 84
Notes 85

6 Comparing the Models 87
6.1 Statistical Issues 87
6.2 Other Criteria 91
6.3 Conclusion 92
Notes 92

Appendix 93
References 95
Index 99

Tables

4.1 Parameter Estimates in the Disequilibrium Model 46
4.2 R²s for the Disequilibrium Model 49
4.3 Excess Demand Forecasts 51
4.4 Natural Unemployment Rates and Vacancy Rates 55
4.5 Impact of Changing the Unionization Rate 57
4.6 Phillips Curve With Alternative Unionization Rates 58
4.7 Impact of Changing the Marginal Income Tax Rate 60

5.1 The Adaptive Expectations Model 77
5.2 The Rational Expectations Model 79
5.3 R²s for the Equilibrium Model 81
5.4 Phillips Curves With Alternative Unionization Rates 82
5.5 Impact of Changing the Marginal Tax Rate 83

6.1 Results of the GSL Estimation of the Hoel Test 91

1

Introduction

1.1 *The Policy Issues*

In 1985, the unemployment rate in the United States was 7.1 percent. There is virtual agreement that unemployment of this magnitude is a serious problem both for the individuals involved and for society as a whole. Workers who lose their jobs bear an immediate financial loss which can be substantial even in the presence of unemployment insurance. Even after a spell of unemployment is completed, an individual may continue to feel its economic effects. Future earnings may be less because of missed opportunities for on-the-job training and other kinds of investment in "human capital." From the point of view of the economy as a whole, perhaps the best way to summarize the impact of unemployment is its cost in foregone output. In 1985, for example, the difference between *actual* Gross National Product and *potential* Gross National Product was roughly $110 billion or 2.75 percent of actual GNP.[1] Finally, we should note that unemployment appears to be related to a number of individual and social problems whose costs are hard to quantify—there is some evidence, for example, that when unemployment goes up, so do heart disease, crime, mental illness, and even suicide.[2]

This monograph discusses several approaches to the analysis of unemployment, and public policy to deal with it. The subject is a complicated one, partially because policy toward unemployment cannot be formulated in isolation from a number of other important issues. Three important related topics are:

1. *Inflation.* If unemployment is such a bad thing, then why can't the government simply hire people who are out of work? Alternatively, why can't the government increase the level of aggregate demand so that private firms will hire more people? As we shall see below, one of the major controversies in macroeconomics is whether

government spending policies can have any impact on unemployment. But it is fairly well agreed that a by-product of government spending policies to decrease unemployment is wage inflation. Hence, one important issue we address is how to estimate the trade-off between inflation and unemployment.

2. *Taxes.* In discussions about unemployment, the subject of tax policy usually arises in two related but distinct contexts. The first is the effect of taxes on aggregate demand. For example, does lowering income taxes induce consumers to spend more, perhaps leading to more employment? The second is the effect of taxes on aggregate supply—do tax decreases affect the amount of work people want to do? If so, can the additional labor supply be absorbed by the economy in a reasonable amount of time? Both of these effects are important and interesting. However, the primary focus of this essay is on the workings of the labor market rather than the determinants of aggregate demand, so we will consider mainly the supply effects of tax changes.[3]

3. *Unionization.* It is usually argued that unions increase unemployment by raising wage rates above their equilibrium level. It could be, however, that the main effect of unions is to reduce the supply of labor, i.e., to shift back the supply curve. This would have the effect of decreasing unemployment. Because both effects might be operative, the outcome is theoretically ambiguous. Indeed, in their very careful analysis of U.S. employment data, Pencavel and Hartsog (1984) find that when it comes to the effect of unionism on relative man-hours worked, the data do not unambiguously point to a negative effect. (p. 217) Our analysis allows the unionization rate to influence the unemployment rate in several different ways; the data determine whether the effect is positive, negative, or zero. We also estimate how changes in the unionization rate would affect the unemployment-inflation trade-off.

1.2 *The Methodological Issues*

Given its evident importance, economists have focused a massive amount of attention on the problem of unemployment. Unfortunately, no consensus has been reached on its causes. A fundamental controversy in the profession is whether unemployment is better viewed as an equilibrium or a disequilibrium phenomenon. Although one may argue about the precise connotation of "equilibrium," for operational purposes we take it to refer to a situation in which prices immediately clear markets: prices are such that neither buyers nor sellers have any reason to attempt to recontract. Applied to the labor market, this means that at each instant the wage rate adjusts so that the supply and demand of labor are equal.

In contrast, the disequilibrium approach views prices as rigid or at least sticky—they do not adjust instantaneously to equalize supply and demand. Hence, suppliers or demanders may have to be rationed, i.e., they cannot obtain as much of a commodity as they desire at the current price. In a disequilibrium labor market, the prevailing wage may be above or below the wage that would equate demand and supply.[4]

Both approaches have advantages and disadvantages. The notion of equilibrium is a cornerstone of economics. It is an enormously useful concept that has permitted a variety of important comparative statics analyses of micro as well as macro phenomena. However, applying the equilibrium paradigm to the analysis of labor market fluctuations leads to an obvious problem—if the supply and demand of labor are always equal, then why is there any unemployment? As Altonji (1982) points out, according to modern equilibrium theorists, the main reason is intertemporal substitution:

> In essence, the [equilibrium] hypothesis explains cyclical fluctuations in employment and unemployment as the response of labour supply to perceived temporary movements in the real wage. The key behavioral postulate is that leisure in the current period is highly substitutable with leisure (and goods) in other periods. Consequently, movements in the current real wage . . . elicit a large labour supply response. (p. 783)

In short, some individuals may *choose* unemployment this year because they believe that they will be able to earn more next year. Is this a sensible story? Critics of the equilibrium view find it implausible that during the Great Depression 25 percent of the workforce was unemployed only because so many people (mistakenly) believed that if they waited a while, they would command a higher wage rate. Nevertheless, proponents of the equilibrium view argue that it provides a good explanation of the historical data. (See, e.g., Lucas and Rapping 1970.) On the other hand, other econometric tests of the equilibrium hypothesis are not very favorable to it. (See Altonji 1982 or Mankiw, *et al.* 1982.)

In contrast, the disequilibrium formulation appears to accommodate the phenomenon of unemployment with relative ease—the wage rate is "too high;" workers without jobs would be happy to work for less, but the wage rate will not fall or, at least, will not fall sufficiently to clear the market. But denial of wage flexibility, simple as that notion may be, brings with it a host of difficulties in model specification and estimation. For example, why do firms pay workers more than the wages required by their potential replacements? After all, by definition, those who are involuntarily unemployed would be willing to work for a wage less than the prevailing one. In short, failure of markets to clear is generally viewed as concomitant with the failure of some agents to optimize.

However, under certain conditions sticky wages can be the outcome of optimizing behavior by both firms and workers. For example, the fact that firms do not always take advantage of opportunities to replace workers with cheaper replacements may be due to costs of labor turnover. Several more sophisticated theoretical attempts to rationalize sticky wages are discussed in section 2.2.3 below. Whatever the success of such theoretical exercises, however, proponents of disequilibrium models are apt to point out that despite difficulties in explaining precisely why the labor market does not clear at every moment in time, the real world does seem to be like that, and this fact should be reflected in economic analysis. As Rees (1970, p. 234) observes,

> Although we know very little about the exact nature of the costs of making wage changes, we can infer that they exist. Wages are, next to house rents, the stickiest general class of prices in the economy, seldom adjusted more frequently than once a year. This stickiness may be reinforced by unionism and collective bargaining, but it was present long before unions arrived.

The debate between protagonists of the equilibrium paradigm and the disequilibrium paradigm has a strong ideological flavor. Proponents of one view frequently think that the alternative view is worthless or perhaps downright silly. A few years ago, one of us gave several seminars on the question of how one would test the null hypothesis that a set of observations is better explained as having been generated from an equilibrium as opposed to a disequilibrium specification. On some of these occasions (mostly in the U.S.), five minutes into the seminar it would be interrupted with the remark, "What you are trying to do is silly, because everybody knows that prices always clear markets and therefore there is nothing to test." At other times (mostly in Europe) the interruption took the form, "What you are trying to do is silly, because everybody knows that prices never clear markets and therefore there is nothing to test." Juxtaposing the two remarks very much convinced us that there definitely is something to test, and that any approach that is not ultimately willing to subject such questions to *data* as the final arbiter must be misguided.

1.3 *Goals of this Monograph*

The equilibrium vs. disequilibrium controversy is not only a matter of methodological interest. Appropriate answers to the important policy problems discussed in the first part of this chapter will depend in part on whether an equilibrium or disequilibrium characterization of the labor market is more appropriate. The goal of this essay is to estimate both disequilibrium and equilibrium models of the U.S. labor market, and to compare the results and their implications for policy. To our knowledge, this is the first attempt to estimate and compare fairly sophisticated equilibrium and disequilibrium labor market models.

A great deal of work in the U.S. labor market has followed the equilibrium paradigm. The economic and statistical issues associated with such models are now well understood, and there is no need for them to be exposed here at great length. In contrast, there has not been a great deal of work based on the disequilibrium paradigm.[5] We shall therefore devote a disproportionate amount of time to discussing the problems that arise in formulating and estimating a disequilibrium model.

Chapter 2 discusses equilibrium and disequilibrium approaches to labor market analysis, with special focus on policy implications. In chapter 3 we specify the disequilibrium model, and in chapter 4 the results are presented and discussed. Chapter 5 contains the equilibrium model. Chapter 6 concludes with comparisons between the disequilibrium and equilibrium results, and some suggestions for future research.

NOTES

[1]This calculation was done using "Okun's Law," which states that for each 1 percentage point reduction in the unemployment rate, real GNP will rise by 2.5 percent. If the actual rate of 7.1 percent had been reduced to an assumed "natural rate" of 6.0 percent, then Okun's Law implies an increase in real GNP of $(7.1 - 6.0) \times 2.5 = 2.75$ percent.

[2]For a careful discussion of the crime issue, see Massourakis, *et al.* (1984).

[3]For a discussion of the influence of tax changes on aggregate demand, see Blinder (1981).

[4]"Disequilibrium" has often been construed to refer to a state in which forces are at work to restore the system to equilibrium. This interpretation is not intended here, since the state of disequilibrium may persist indefinitely. For this reason, disequilibrium in the present sense is sometimes called a "fix-price equilibrium."

[5]For some examples, see Rosen and Quandt (1978), Romer (1981), and Artus, Laroque, and Michel (1984).

2

Equilibrium vs. Disequilibrium Labor Market Analysis

In this chapter we discuss how labor markets have been treated in equilibrium and disequilibrium contexts. As preface, two points should be emphasized. First, we consider only analyses that deal with both supply and demand in the *labor market as a whole*. Thus, we exclude from discussion the very interesting disequilibrium analyses that have been done of *individual* labor supply decisions without explicit reference to the demand side of the market. (See, e.g., Ham 1982 and Dickens and Lundberg 1985.)

Second, it is important to distinguish between the use of the term "disequilibrium" in this monograph and its use in some previous work. As noted in chapter 1, we characterize as disequilibrium a situation in which price fails to clear a market. Hence, some agents face rationing—they cannot obtain all of the commodity they desire at the going price. This usage is widespread and in conformity with much of the literature, e.g., Barro and Grossman (1971), Fair and Jaffee (1972), and Malinvaud (1976). In contrast, some authors characterize a situation as being in disequilibrium if the actors fail to reach an optimum in a given period, even though in each period prices adjust so as to bring supply and demand towards equality. (See, e.g., Nadiri and Rosen 1973, Chow 1977, and Sarantis 1981.) Thus, according to this partial adjustment approach, any model in which either prices or quantities (or both) adjust slowly in each period toward their long-run values is in disequilibrium. There is no point in engaging in a semantic discussion of which is the "real" meaning of disequilibrium. Suffice it to say that very different maintained hypotheses are involved.

2.1 *Equilibrium Labor Market Analysis*

The biggest problem that equilibrium models of the labor market have is explaining the existence of unemployment. In some equilibrium models, this problem is "solved" by ignoring the existence of unemployment. For example, Lewis (1963) and Pencavel and Hartsog (1984) examine the effects of unionism on wage rates and hours of work in a two-sector model of the labor market. The wage rate clears the labor market each year. No unemployment equation is grafted onto the analysis of wages and hours. From the point of view of public policy toward unemployment, what do such models tell us? Given that they make no attempt to deal with unemployment, the answer has to be "nothing."

In contrast, the classic equilibrium model by Lucas and Rapping (L-R) (1970) explicitly considers unemployment. A detailed discussion of the L-R model is provided in chapter 5. For the moment, we merely describe its main components. The aggregate supply of labor depends upon current and anticipated wages and prices, the interest rate, and the market value of household assets. The demand side of the model is derived from the marginal productivity condition for a constant elasticity of substitution production function. There is *no* disequilibrium in the model: "The current wage is assumed to equate quantity demanded and quantity supplied each period" (Lucas and Rapping 1970, p. 272). Nevertheless, L-R do allow for unemployment, and posit that it is due to job search and erroneous wage-price expectations. Using this theory of unemployment and making certain simplifying assumptions, L-R complete their model with an equation that relates the unemployment rate to current and lagged wages and prices, and to the lagged unemployment rate.

In both the supply and demand equations, L-R exercise great care to account for slow adjustment in behavior. In spite of this, they take as a maintained hypothesis that the labor market itself is always in equilibrium and that there is no lag in the response of the real wage to changes in supply and demand.

From a policy point of view, two points are worth noting:

1. The model does allow for a short-run trade-off between inflation and unemployment. This is possible because, by inflating wages (via aggregate demand policy), the government can temporarily fool workers into believing that their real wage has increased. Note, however, that if one augments the L-R theory with rational expectations—i.e., workers' expectations are on average correct predictors of

the future—then the model implies that there is not even a short-run trade-off between inflation and unemployment.

2. Unionization is ignored in the model. L-R correctly note that theoretically, changes in the unionization rate have an ambiguous effect upon the level of wages in the economy as a whole. If unions increase the wage rate in the union sector, some workers may have to seek jobs in the nonunion sector. But the influx of workers into the nonunion sector may depress wages there, so the impact on the average wage level is unclear. However, just because the overall impact is ambiguous does not mean that it is zero. Unionization should at least be considered for a role in the models of the labor market.

2.2 Disequilibrium Labor Market Analysis

2.2.1 Disequilibrium and the IS-LM Model

It is useful to begin our discussion of disequilibrium by considering the standard "Keynesian" IS-LM model. In the current context, a key point is that despite the fact that one often thinks of Keynesian analysis as being "disequilibrium," in IS-LM analysis virtually all markets clear. After all, the IS curve is the locus of equilibrium points in the goods market; the LM curve is the locus of equilibrium points in the money market; and their intersection is a point of general equilibrium.

The intersection of the IS and LM curves determines real output and the interest rate. Where does unemployment come in? According to the model, changes in output drive changes in employment. As suggested in a popular elementary textbook: "Faster growth of real output naturally means faster growth in the number of jobs and, hence, lower unemployment. Conversely, slower growth of real output means slower growth in the number of jobs and, hence, higher unemployment" (Baumol and Blinder 1985, p. 311). Contrary to what this statement implies, however, it is not "natural" that changes in output will change the unemployment rate—if wages are perfectly flexible in the labor market, then there will be no unemployment, regardless of the level of output.[1] In short, the IS-LM model appears to be an equilibrium model of output and interest rate determination with a disequilibrium model of the labor market grafted onto it.

2.2.2 *The Barro-Grossman Model*

These inadequacies of the standard IS-LM model led Barro and Grossman (B-G) (1971) to study the theoretical properties of a model which allowed for price rigidities in *all* markets. Again, we will make no attempt to summarize their entire analysis. We merely want to provide enough of the flavor of their work to make the following point: Theory shows that counter-intuitive results with respect to the efficacy of various economic policies can arise in disequilibrium models. Therefore, as an empirical matter, it is important to find out whether disequilibria exist in various markets.

To begin, B-G consider a profit-maximizing firm employing labor as its only input. Suppose that the firm believes that it can hire all the labor it desires at the going real wage (W/P), and can sell all the output it supplies at the going price (P). Then profit maximization leads to an optimal quantity of labor hired L^D, and an associated optimal quantity of output supplied, Q^S. Supplies and demands which are based on the assumption that there will be no rationing are referred to as being "notional."

Now suppose that the (rigid) price in the output market is such that there is excess supply. Given the principle of voluntary exchange, according to which no purchaser can be forced to buy more and no seller to sell more than he or she wants, the quantity actually sold, Q, will be the minimum of the quantity supplied and the quantity demanded; in this case, then, $Q < Q^S$. Facing this constraint, how does the firm decide how much labor to hire? It simply hires the minimum quantity required to produce Q; call it $\hat{L}^D$. Hence, the constraint $Q < Q^S$ implies that $\hat{L}^D < L^D$. What is remarkable about all of this is that the effective demand for labor can change even if the real wage stays constant. "The quantity of employment . . . is not uniquely associated with the real wage" (Barro and Grossman 1971, p. 86).

Some further implications of the model can be obtained by referring to figure 2.1. The horizontal axis measures the quantity of labor; the vertical axis measures the real wage rate; L^D is the notional demand for labor, and L^S is the notional supply of labor. If $Q = Q^S$, L^D is the effective demand for labor. If $Q < Q^S$, the effective demand for labor, $\hat{L}^D$, is independent of the real wage; this possibility is depicted by the vertical line AB.

Figure 2.1*

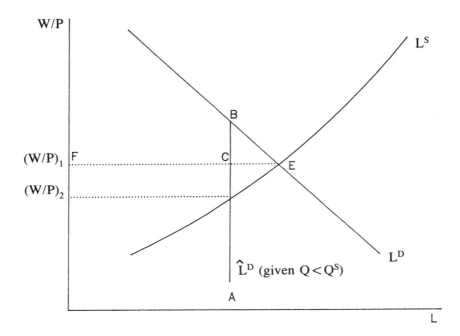

*Based on figure 1 in Barro and Grossman (1971), p. 86.

Suppose that initially $Q^S = Q$, so that equilibrium in the labor market is determined by the intersection of L^D and L^S at point E, which is associated with a real wage of $(W/P)_1$. Now say that there is a shock to the system which leads to the current price level being too high to clear the goods market. In this case, $Q < Q^S$, and the labor demand schedule is $\hat{L}^D$. Assuming that the real wage is rigid at $(W/P)_1$, the quantity of labor supplied, FE, exceeds the quantity demanded (FC) by the distance CE, which represents the amount of involuntary unemployment. Thus, involuntary unemployment is *not* a consequence of the real wage being "too high."

Suppose now that a fall in the real wage to $(W/P)_2$ were engineered. Now there would be no involuntary unemployment. However, the quantity of labor hired would still be suboptimal in the sense of being

CE less than the quantity associated with general equilibrium. From a policy perspective, the important result is that programs designed to lower the real wage will not necessarily be the "cure" when the level of employment is smaller than that associated with the general equilibrium solution. In this example, the "fault" is due to inadequate commodity demand, and the "cure" is to stimulate the goods market.

Of course, this need not be the case; for other configurations of supply and demand in the goods and labor markets, real wage reduction may be efficacious in reducing unemployment. Moreover, a complete analysis should consider disequilibria in both markets simultaneously. But for our purposes, the basic point has been made: policy prescriptions that are appropriate in a world with flexible prices and wages may be quite different from those which make sense when prices and wages are fixed.

2.2.3 Theories of Nonmarket-Clearing Wages

B-G's model begs the question of why wages are rigid, even in the short run. As noted above, this is sometimes viewed as the Achilles' heel of disequilibrium models, because it seems to imply the absence of optimizing behavior. The purpose of this section is to give some examples of the theorizing that has been done to rationalize the existence of fixed wages.

a. *Efficiency Wages.* Our exposition of this model closely follows Yellen (1984), but we change her notation to match ours.

Suppose that all workers are identical, and the amount of output produced by a worker depends on his effort, e, which in turn depends upon his real wage, W/P. We denote this functional dependence by $e(W/P)$. The number of "efficiency" units employed by the firm is the number of workers hired, L^D, times the effort per worker, or $e(W/P)L^D$. If labor is the *only input,* then firm output, Q, is given by $Q = F[e(W/P)L^D]$, where $F[\cdot]$ is the production function. The firm has to choose optimal values of W/P and L^D; call them $(W/P)^\dagger$ and $L^{D\dagger}$, respectively. The first order condition for profit maximization with respect to W/P implies that $(W/P)^\dagger$ should be set such that the elasticity of effort with respect to the real wage is unity.[2] For a given $(W/P)^\dagger$, the number of workers hired is set so that the value of the marginal product of a worker is equal to his wage: $e(W/P)^\dagger F'[e(W/P)^\dagger L^{D\dagger}] = (W/P)^\dagger$, that is to say, the number of efficiency units embodied in a worker times the marginal product of each efficiency unit equals the worker's real wage.

Now, it is possible that $(W/P)^\dagger$ may exceed labor's reservation wage. Unemployed workers would therefore be willing to work for a lower wage, but firms will not find it profitable to hire them. Why not? Because any reduction in the wage rate would lower the productivity of those already employed.

The model also has something to say about the existence of a rigid real wage, i.e., why shocks that change the marginal product of labor tend to alter employment but not $(W/P)^\dagger$. To see this, simply note that shifts in the marginal product of labor will not change the condition that determines the real wage, i.e., that the elasticity of effort with respect to the wage must equal one. See Yellen (1984) and footnote 2 for further details and references.

b. *Dual Labor Markets.* Salop (1979) develops a model in which individual workers and firms face some uncertainty, although there is no uncertainty in the aggregate. Workers are uncertain about the nonpecuniary aspects of various jobs; they learn about these characteristics only by experience, and may quit if they think they can do better elsewhere. The firm can replace workers who quit, but must pay "training costs" in connection with the new workers.

Let E be the employment of the firm, N the new hires, q the quit rate, w the wage, and z a measure of general labor market conditions (e.g., the average wage in the economy taking into account the ease of getting a job). Quits are assumed to depend on the wage *relative to* general labor market tightness,

$$q = q(w/z)$$

with $q' < 0$ and $q'' > 0$. In a stationary state, it must be true that the size of the firm does not change; hence N must equal $q(w/z)E$—new hires equal the actual number of quits.

The firm's problem is to select employment E, new hires N and the wage w, so as to maximize profits, taking into account the fact that more new hires entail higher training costs. As expected, the solution of this optimization problem yields expressions for E, N, and w in terms of the only variable in the system that is exogenous to the firm, z: $E = E(z)$, with $E' < 0$; $w/z = W(z)$, with $W' < 0$; and $N = N(z)$ with an unsigned derivative.

If we now assume that n firms operate in the economy, we can write down economy-wide equilibrium conditions that determine the equilibrium values of z and n. The key result is that this equilibrium may well be characterized by involuntary unemployment over and above the frictional level of unemployment.

The intuitive basis for this finding is that new and old workers are paid the same wage in the model. Thus, if there are n firms, there are in general n wages that can perform market clearing. However, each firm has two "markets" that need to be cleared; an internal market which determines employment and quits, and an external one which determines new hires. As Salop points out, "Since there are only n prices attempting to clear 2n markets, it is not surprising that quantity rationing must serve as the clearing device in some markets, leading to the possibility of unemployment at the equilibrium." (p. 121)

c. *Implicit Contracts.* Textbook models of the labor market view it as a spot market—each period the wage clears the market, thereby equating the marginal revenue product of labor with the wage. A number of writers (see Azariadis 1975 or Baily 1974) have argued that it is more appropriate to view the wage setting process as being governed by long-term contracts between employee and employer. The "contracts" are not written down and legally binding; rather, they are *implicit* agreements that are maintained because both sides have incentives to continue the relationship.

Why do such implicit contracts arise? Workers are faced with uncertain streams of income, and it is very difficult for them to shed this risk by purchasing private insurance. One possible way for the workers to reduce risk is to pass some of it to firms through long-term contracts which reduce the sensitivity of wages to demand fluctuations. Thus, when times are (unexpectedly) good, workers will receive a real wage that is less than their marginal revenue product. Conversely, when times are (unexpectedly) bad, the real wage exceeds the marginal product. The difference between the marginal revenue product and the wage when times are good can be thought of as an insurance premium which finances the higher than marginal revenue product wage when times are bad. As long as the firm is less risk averse than its workers, it pays for the firm to enter into such arrangements—it will be able to pay workers less on average because the workers value the insurance being provided by the firm. Again, then, there is nothing necessarily irrational about rigid wages.

Summary. Recent theoretical developments have gone a long way toward explaining the stickiness of real wages. As Azariadis and Stiglitz (1983) and Lindbeck and Snower (1985) note, there are still many problems with these models. In particular, in implicit contract models it is difficult to explain convincingly just why sticky wages are associated with unemployment. (This is because in some of these models a *low* sticky wage is the price paid by workers for greater employment security.) However, enough theoretical work on the consistency of sticky wages and rational behavior has been done so that nonmarket-clearing models should not be dismissed out of hand.

NOTES

[1]We are, of course, ignoring the "search unemployment" discussed in section 2.1 above.

[2]Real profits, π, can be written $\pi = F(e(W/P)L^D) - \dfrac{W}{P} L^D$. The firm's first order conditions for profit maximization are

$$\frac{\partial \pi}{\partial (W/P)} = F'e'L^D - L^D = 0 \tag{i}$$

$$\frac{\partial \pi}{\partial L^D} = F'e - \frac{W}{P} = 0. \tag{ii}$$

Equation (i) implies

$$F'e' = 1; \tag{iii}$$

Equation (ii) implies

$$\frac{W}{P} = F'e. \tag{iv}$$

Multiplying both sides of (iv) by e'/e yields $\dfrac{W}{P}\dfrac{e'}{e} = F'e'$, which equals 1 by equation (iii). But $\dfrac{W}{P}\dfrac{e'}{e}$ is the required elasticity, so the result is proven.

3

Formulating a Disequilibrium Model

3.1 *Introductory Remarks*

In this section we specify an estimable disequilibrium model of the labor market. Before discussing each equation of the model, it is important to answer two general questions.

i. *Why study just the labor market?* The theoretical discussion in chapter 2 indicated that the interaction between various markets can have important consequences for the efficacy of macroeconomic policy. Does it not follow that a general disequilibrium model should be estimated? The problem with that strategy is a practical one. As will be seen below, the technology of estimating disequilibrium models is sufficiently difficult that, given currently available computational methods, estimating a general disequilibrium model is extremely difficult. This is particularly true if the individual markets are to be modeled in some detail. A start has to be made somewhere; we believe that careful analysis of one market in disequilibrium is a good beginning.

Given that technological considerations impel a partial disequilibrium analysis, why choose the labor market, rather than the goods or money markets? We think that from the point of view of achieving results that may be useful from a policy point of view, the labor market is most important. To see why, note that many economists agree that if some kind of shock moves the economy away from a full employment equilibrium, there are self-correcting mechanisms that will *eventually* restore the system to full employment. The crucial question for designing policy is, how long do we have to wait? If the labor market responds quickly to shocks in the sense that excess supply quickly brings down wages, then one does not need to wait very long. Activist macroeconomic policies are not required. Conversely, if wages tend to be very rigid, then such policies may be useful. We think that a key issue dividing "Keynesians" and "neoclassicists" is how well the labor market works.

More than 40 years ago, Modigliani (1944) noted that economists' understanding of the labor market appeared to be the weak link in comprehending macroeconomic phenomena.[1] It is still true today, which is why the labor market seems a natural focus for our attention.

ii. *Must the model have "choice-theoretic foundations"?* As a methodological stance, it is now widely agreed that equations in econometric models should have "choice-theoretic foundations." This means that the behavioral relations should be based on optimizing behavior by various agents. It is hard to disagree with this prescription for rigor in modeling, and to the extent possible, we have tried to follow it. Nevertheless, there are at least two reasons why it is not sensible to make a fetish out of choice-theoretic foundations. These points, incidentally, apply equally well to equilibrium and disequilibrium models.

First, virtually all that theory tells us about is the decisions of individual units, either firms or people. If we seek to explain market phenomena, the decision rules of these individuals must be aggregated. However, even if a rigorously derived equation explains the behavior of an individual, it is only in very special (and unlikely) cases that the same functional form will correctly describe aggregate behavior. Unfortunately, equations for aggregate behavior carefully derived by adding up those for individuals are usually econometrically intractable. The usual solution is to assume that individuals in the aggregate act "as if" they were a single optimizing individual. Thus, for example, the aggregate demand curve for labor is customarily derived as if there were one firm with a particular production function. This is a convenient fiction, which helps to inject some discipline into the modeling process by narrowing the set of explanatory variables, aiding in the choice of functional form, etc. Still, it *is* a fiction, and the fact that the estimates of the parameters of an "aggregate individual" equation may not be consistent with constraints imposed by individual maximization is not necessarily damning.

Second, sometimes there are simply no choice-theoretic foundations upon which to build. For example, it is commonly assumed that for a market out of equilibrium the rate of price change is proportional to the discrepancy between quantity supplied and quantity demanded (See e.g., Samuelson 1970). This is a convenient formulation, but why should it be true? One might argue as follows. Assume that there exist demand and supply functions $D(p_t)$, $S(p_t)$ depending on current price. If the economic system behaved *as if* it incurred certain costs whenever prices change (adjustment costs) and whenever demand failed to equal supply (disequilibrium costs), one might think of the system as minimizing a cost function $C = \theta_1(p_t - p_{t-1})^2 + \theta_2(D(p_t) - S(p_t))^2$. Differentiating this with respect to p_t and setting equal to zero yields an equation of the form $p_t - p_{t-1} = \gamma(D(p_t) - S(p_t))$ if demand and supply are both linear. This appears to justify the assumption that price change is proportional to excess demand, but one cannot avoid asking why we should think of the economic system acting so as to minimize the cost C. Investigators are thus forced to use such *ad hoc* specifications because there is currently no satisfactory theory of adjustment costs, and how they influence the rate of price change.

3.2 *The Disequilibrium Model*[2]

Our model consists of six equations, one each for the marginal productivity of labor, the supply of labor, the observed quantity of labor, nominal wages, the price level, and the vacancy-unemployment rate relationship. The deterministic version of each equation is discussed in turn. We defer until section 3.3 the matter of stochastic specification.

Marginal Productivity of Labor. A necessary condition for profit maximization requires that the marginal product of labor equal the real wage:

$$(W_t/P_t) = f_L(L_t, K_t, t) \qquad (3.2.1)$$

where f_L is the partial derivative of the production function,

$$Q_t = f(L_t, K_t, t), \qquad (3.2.2)$$

and where Q_t is output, L_t is man-hours of labor,[3] K_t is the flow of services of capital, and t is a time trend representing the state of technical progress in period t. Solving (3.2.1) for K_t, substituting this into (3.2.2), assuming that the resulting equation can be solved for L_t, and calling the quantity of labor demanded D_t, yields

$$D_t = D((W_t/P_t),Q_t,t). \tag{3.2.3}$$

Although (3.2.3) is a proper structural relationship, it is not a reduced form equation and hence not in the usual form for the demand equation because of the appearance of the endogenous variable Q_t on the right hand side. It also appears desirable to assume that the notional and actual output variables coincide and may thus both be symbolized by Q_t.

Equation (3.2.3) assumes that the demand for labor adjusts instantaneously to change in output; we can allow for the possibility of lags in the process by positing

$$D_t = D((W_t/P_t),Q_t,Q_{t-1},t).$$

For purposes of estimation, a log-linear approximation (except for t) is employed:[4]

$$\ell n\, D_t = \alpha_0 + \alpha_1 \ell n(W_t/P_t) + \alpha_2 \ell n Q_t$$
$$+ \alpha_3 \ell n Q_{t-1} + \alpha_4 t. \tag{3.2.4}$$

Formulation (3.2.4) (or a minor variant) is a common starting point for both equilibrium and disequilibrium studies of labor markets (see, for example, Lucas and Rapping 1970, Rosen and Quandt 1978, Romer 1981, Smyth (undated), Hajivassiliou 1983 and Bernanke 1984.) Nevertheless, ideally one would want to study a multimarket model in which output was treated econometrically as an endogenous variable. This task is beyond the scope of the current study, and for tractability it will be assumed that output is exogenous.

Supply of Labor. The total number of man-hours supplied in year t depends upon the real *net* wage, (W_{nt}/P_t), and the potential labor force, H_t, which is essentially a scale variable to capture the effect of population growth. Again assuming a log-linear specification:

$$\ell n S_t = \beta_0 + \beta_1 \ell n(W_{nt}/P_t) + \beta_2 \ell n H_t \tag{3.2.5}$$

where S_t denotes notional supply. The basic theory of labor supply suggests that nonlabor income belongs in equation (3.2.5). However, Romer (1981) pointed out that unearned income is endogenous in a life cycle model of labor supply determination, and shows that more sensible results can be obtained when it is omitted.

Equation (3.2.5) ignores the impact that unions might have upon the supply of labor. Specifically, it has been argued that some unions have "forced employers to agree to hire only union workers, thereby giving the union virtually complete control of the supply of labor. Then, by following restrictive membership practices—long apprenticeships, exorbitant initiation fees, the limitation or flat prohibition of new members—the union causes an artificial restriction in the labor supply" (McConnell 1966, p. 562). To explore whether or not such a unionization effect is present, we augment (3.2.5) with a variable $UNION_t$, the proportion of the labor force that is unionized:

$$\ell nS_t = \beta_0 + \beta_1 \ell n(W_{nt}/P_t) + \beta_2 \ell nH_t$$

$$+ \beta_3 UNION_t. \tag{3.2.6}$$

Note that equation (3.2.6) ignores the possible roles of intertemporal labor supply substitution and expectations concerning future labor market conditions. From a logical point of view, there is nothing to prevent a careful examination of expectational issues in the context of a disequilibrium model; indeed, this has been attempted by Eaton and Quandt (1983) and Hall, et al. (1985). Nevertheless, since most of the "action" in explaining unemployment in equilibrium models comes from expectations, we felt that a sharper comparison of the two approaches would be possible if expectational issues were not stressed in the disequilibrium model. We note in passing, however, that for at least some simple expectational models the main implication is that the lagged wage as well as its current value appear in the supply equation. When we augmented equation (3.2.6) with the lagged real net wage, we found that it did not have much of an impact on the other parameter values.

Observed Quantity of Labor. In an equilibrium model, the observed quantity of labor is determined by the intersection of the supply and demand curves. In a disequilibrium model, this is not the case. In conformity with most of the work in disequilibrium theory, we assume that the quantity observed is the minimum of the quantities supplied and demanded at the current wage:

$$\ell nL_t = \min (\ell nS_t, \ell nD_t). \qquad (3.2.7)$$

Equation (3.2.7) is perhaps the most distinctive component of the disequilibrium model. The fact that in any given year the observed quantity of labor is on either the supply or demand curve—but *a priori* we don't know which one—accounts for most of the statistical problems associated with disequilibrium models.

In this context, it is useful to recall from chapter 2 that some writers have characterized a model as "disequilibrium" merely if prices and/or quantities fail to achieve their long-run values in any given period. As Chow (1977) shows, such models can be estimated by garden variety simultaneous equations methods. In our opinion, however, the failure of markets to clear, which is central to the theoretical disequilibrium models discussed in section 2.2, is the essential aspect of the disequilibrium phenomenon, and must be dealt with head on.

Clearly, equation (3.2.7) does not describe completely what is presumably a very complicated rationing story. It has been pointed out (Muellbauer 1977, and Hajivassiliou 1983) that a formulation such as (3.2.7) may represent some misspecification in situations in which the aggregate labor market is, in effect, the sum of many individual submarkets. If some of these exhibit excess demand while others, at the same time, have excess supply, the observed transacted quantity can be shown to be strictly less than either aggregate demand or aggregate supply. The appropriate econometric estimating method depends very much on how one assumes the aggregation of submarkets is accomplished. Quandt (1986) has shown that for at least one broad class of aggregation procedures, the theoretically misspecified procedure based on the simple "min condition" still gives acceptable results. In any event, the "min condition" helps keep the problem tractable, and we are assuming that the misspecification involved in (3.2.7) is not too serious in practice.

Nominal Wage Adjustment. Thus far, our model says little about how the history of wage and price movements affects the current nominal wage. Standard models of "sluggish" behavior imply that the current value of a particular variable will depend on its past values; hence, we expect W_t to depend on its past values. Similarly, lagged prices are included because of the expectation that workers' nominal wage requests will depend on the extent of recent price changes. *Ceteris paribus,* higher prices will result in high nominal wages. (Indeed, in much of the union sector, indexing is formally built into wage contracts.) As usual, theory does not give much guidance with respect to the pattern of lags; the specification reported below was superior to several alternatives in the sense of leading to the best fit to the data.

We also included in the nominal wage equation the official unemployment rate, U_t, and the change in the unionization rate, $\Delta UNION_t$. The presence of the official unemployment rate reflects the possibility that when the labor market is slack (high U_t), then nominal wages will be lower, *ceteris paribus,* and vice versa. The change in unionization variable allows for the possibility that unions can exogenously raise the nominal wage above the level that otherwise would have obtained. The change in the unionization rate rather than its level reflects the assumption that an increase in unionization induces a once-and-for-all increase in the nominal wage; all of the union's "monopoly power" is exploited immediately.

We can summarize the preceding discussion of the determinants of the nominal wage with the following equation:

$$\ell nW_t = \gamma_0 + \gamma_1 \ell nW_{t-1} + \gamma_2 U_t$$
$$+ \gamma_3(\ell nP_t - \ell nP_{t-1})$$
$$+ \gamma_4(\ell nP_{t-1} - \ell nP_{t-2})$$
$$+ \gamma_5 \ell nW_{t-2}$$
$$+ \gamma_6 \Delta UNION_t. \tag{3.2.8}$$

One final issue concerns the use of U_t as a measure of slackness in the labor market. It is well known that unemployment as measured in the official statistical series does not correspond well to the theoretical notion of unemployment as the inability to find work at the going wage. (See the discussion of the vacancy-unemployment relationship below.) Why not, then, include excess demand, $(\ell nD_t - \ell nS_t)$, rather than U_t? The choice of U_t reflects the fact that workers and employers do not know $(\ell nD_t - \ell nS_t)$; they have to rely on their perceptions of the labor market situation, and these are well measured by U_t. Indeed, when we estimated the model including $(\ell nD_t - \ell nS_t)$ instead of U_t, implausible parameter estimates resulted.

Price Adjustment. The price level of this period depends upon the lagged price level and the recent history of nominal wage changes:

$$\ell nP_t = \delta_0 + \delta_1 \ell nP_{t-1} + \delta_2(\ell nW_t - \ell nW_{t-1})$$

$$+ \delta_3(\ell nW_{t-1} - \ell nW_{t-2})$$

$$+ \delta_4(\ell nPF_t - \ell nPF_{t-1}) + \delta_5 t, \qquad (3.2.9)$$

where PF_t is a price index for energy in period t. The lagged price term reflects sluggishness in the price adjustment process. Lagged nominal wages are included because producers take factor costs into account when setting their prices. (Such behavior is consistent with, for example, simple mark-up models of pricing behavior.) The presence of the energy price variable is responsive to the suggestion of Gordon (1982) and others that macroeconomic price equations be augmented with variables to account for "price shocks" which exogenously affect prices. (Note that because we do not attempt to model disequilibrium in the goods market, excess demand does not appear in (3.2.9).)

Vacancy-Unemployment Relationship. Let V_t be the vacancy rate defined as the ratio of vacancies to the total labor force in year t, and U_t be the official unemployment rate, both measured as fractions. Ignore for the moment that U_t does not measure correctly the discrepancy between the amount of labor supplied and the amount workers desire to supply at the prevailing wage. Then by definition, $D_t = L_t(1 + V_t)$ and $S_t = L_t(1 + U_t)$, which imply

$$\frac{D_t}{S_t} = \frac{1 + V_t}{1 + U_t}.$$

Taking logarithms,

$$\ell nD_t - \ell nS_t = \ell n(1 + V_t) - \ell n(1 + U_t).$$

If V_t and U_t are fairly small, then a Taylor Series approximation gives us

$$\ell n D_t - \ell n S_t = V_t - U_t. \qquad (3.2.10)$$

Unfortunately, U.S. annual data for the vacancy rate do not exist for our sample period. Pencavel (1974) suggests that the vacancy rate is a stable function of the unemployment rate which can be approximated by the hyperbolic relationship[5]

$$V_t = \lambda / U_t, \qquad (3.2.11)$$

where λ is a parameter. Substituting into (3.2.10) leads to

$$\ell n D_t - \ell n S_t = \frac{\lambda}{U_t} - U_t. \qquad (3.2.12)$$

Equation (3.2.12) gives the relationship between the official unemployment rate and the excess demand for labor. It does not hold as an identity for three reasons. First, equation (3.2.10) holds as an approximation. Second, equation (3.2.11) holds only as an approximation as well. Third, it is likely that U_t measures the "true" unemployment rate with error. As Lucas and Rapping (1970, p. 272) note:

> The government generates an unemployment series based on the number of people who answer yes to the question: Are you actually seeking work? There is strong temptation to assume that respondents to this survey take the question to mean, Are you seeking work at the current wage rate?, but it is important to recognize that this assumption is simply a hypothesis, the truth of which is far from obvious.

Indeed, one possible way to interpret equation (3.2.12) is not as a "vacancies equation," but simply as a way to summarize the relationship between the excess demand for labor and the official unemployment rate.

3.3 Econometric Issues

In this section we give a brief introduction to the problems of estimation in the context of both equilibrium and disequilibrium models. Estimation in equilibrium models is well understood and our treatment here can be brief; however, we cannot omit it altogether because both the similarities (such as they are) and the more important differences between the two cases are instructive. In order to highlight these and to avoid getting bogged down in the details of our actual models, we concentrate on some general formulations that do not have concrete economic content.

The Equilibrium Model. Consider a single market for a hypothetical good. The market demand for this good in period t, D_t, is derived by aggregating individual consumers' demand curves. The individual demand curves, in turn, are the outcome when consumers maximize their utility functions subject to a budget constraint. Under a variety of circumstances, it is reasonable to approximate market demand linearly as

$$D_t = \alpha_1 p_t + \beta_1' x_{1t} + u_{1t} \qquad (3.3.1)$$

where p_t is the price, α_1 is an (unknown) coefficient, $\beta_1' x_{1t}$ is shorthand for $\beta_{11} x_{11t} + \beta_{12} x_{12t} + \ldots + \beta_{1k} x_{1kt}$ and expresses the effect on demand of certain other variables that are external (exogenous or predetermined) to the key variables of interest, and u_{1t} is an error term, intrinsically unobservable but nevertheless there, that expresses errors of specification and measurement. Similarly, producers' supply is derived by maximizing their profit (or whatever other objective is appropriate in the institutional setting considered) subject to the production function which constrains the manner in which inputs can be transformed into outputs. After aggregation we can write

$$S_t = \alpha_2 p_t + \beta_2' x_{2t} + u_{2t} \qquad (3.3.2)$$

where x_{2t} denotes the exogenous and predetermined variables appropriate to the determination of supply. As usual, $\beta_1' x_{1t}$ and $\beta_2' x_{2t}$ both include a constant term.

The key feature of the equilibrium model is that the observer's measurements on the key items, price and quantity traded, always correspond to equilibrium values. Under these circumstances $D_t = S_t$ and we can assign the common label Y_t. Equations (3.3.1) and (3.3.2) then become

$$Y_t = \alpha_1 p_t + \beta_1' x_{1t} + u_{1t}. \qquad (3.3.3)$$

$$Y_t = \alpha_2 p_t + \beta_2' x_{2t} + u_{2t}. \qquad (3.3.4)$$

The problem of estimation then is this: given data on Y_t, p_t and on the additional variables x_{1t}, x_{2t}, how do we obtain reasonable guesses for the unknown coefficients α_1, β_1, α_2, β_2?

All the estimation problems share the characteristic that a model must be specified and more or less extensive assumptions must be made about it. In the present case this includes the specification of the mathematical form of the equations (3.3.3) and (3.3.4); it includes the assumption that variables x_{1t}, x_{2t} are predetermined, i.e., that their statistical properties or behavior depend neither on Y_t and p_t nor on the coefficients α_1, β_1, α_2, β_2; and finally it includes some assumption about the statistical behavior of the error terms u_{1t}, u_{2t} (e.g., that the population of error terms has zero mean, perhaps constant variance, perhaps that the values of u_{1t}, u_{2t} do not depend on previously obtained values for some other time period, and so on). Any one of these assumptions could, of course, be in error and there are systematic procedures (specification tests) with which the validity of the assumptions can be investigated. But apart from that, two features need to be noted: (1) Any method of estimation that is appropriate to a model will produce "good" estimates, i.e., estimates that have desirable statistical properties such as unbiasedness (in rare instances) or consistency and efficiency, only to the extent that reality corresponds to the assumptions of the model. (2) If reality does correspond to the model's assumption, we are literally acting as if "nature" generated observations on the jointly dependent variables Y_t and p_t according to the following "algorithm." First, nature, knowing the values of all the coefficients and all the x's, computes $\beta_1' x_{1t}$ and $\beta_2' x_{2t}$. Next, nature draws randomly two error terms u_{1t}, u_{2t} from the appropriate statistical distribution. Denoting for simplicity $\beta_1' x_{1t} + u_{1t}$ by c_1 and $\beta_2' x_{2t} + u_{2t}$ by c_2, nature then solves the pair of simultaneous linear equations:

$$Y_t - \alpha_1 p_t = c_1$$
$$Y_t - \alpha_2 p_t = c_2$$

for Y_t and p_t, and then allows us to see the solution values.

As is well known, there are numerous ways to estimate such a model (see Chow 1983, chapter 5). Although it may seem tempting to apply ordinary least squares, equation by equation, that is an undesirable method since it produces inconsistent estimates. However, two-stage and three-stage least squares and several other methods are appropriate.

Here we briefly review only one particular method, full information maximum likelihood. We do so partly because it has extremely desirable properties and partly because in disequilibrium models it is frequently the only practicable method; thus the comparison is of some interest.

We start out by assuming that the error terms u_{1t}, u_{2t} are jointly normally distributed. For the sake of conceptual and notational simplicity we consider a "bare bones" case: (i) the statistical distribution of u_{1t}, u_{2t} is identical for all values of t; (ii) the expected values of u_{1t}, u_{2t} are zero. Now define the *joint density function* of u_{1t} and u_{2t}, $f(u_{1t},u_{2t})$, as the function which shows the probability that any particular combination of u_{1t} and u_{2t} will occur.[6] Given assumptions (i) and (ii), it can be shown that

$$f(u_{1t},u_{2t}) = \frac{1}{2\pi(\sigma_1^2\sigma_2^2 - \sigma_{12}^2)^{1/2}} \exp\left\{ -\frac{1}{2(\sigma_1^2\sigma_2^2 - \sigma_{12}^2)} \right.$$

$$\left. \left[\sigma_2^2 u_{1t}^2 + \sigma_1^2 u_{2t}^2 - 2\sigma_{12}u_{1t}u_{2t}\right]\right\} \tag{3.3.5}$$

where σ_1^2, σ_2^2 are the variances of u_{1t}, u_{2t} and σ_{12} is the covariance between them. Using the definition of u_{1t} and u_{2t} from equations (3.3.3) and (3.3.4), we can obtain from equation (3.3.5) the joint density of Y_t, p_t (which are also random variables). This density is

$$h(Y_t,p_t) = \frac{|\alpha_1 - \alpha_2|}{2\pi(\sigma_1^2\sigma_2^2 - \sigma_{12}^2)^{1/2}} \exp\left\{ -\frac{1}{2(\sigma_1^2\sigma_2^2 - \sigma_{12}^2)} \right.$$

$$\left[\sigma_2^2(Y_t-\alpha_1 p_t-\beta_1' x_{1t})^2 + \sigma_1^2(Y_t-\alpha_2 p_t-\beta_2' x_{2t})^2\right.$$

$$\left.\left. - 2\sigma_{12}(Y_t-\alpha_1 p_t-\beta_1' x_{1t})(Y_t-\alpha_2 p_t-\beta_2' x_{2t})\right]\right\}. \tag{3.3.6}$$

The term $|\alpha_1 - \alpha_2|$ is the Jacobian of the transformation from the u's to (Y_t, p_t); for a rationale for its presence, see appendix 3.1 In the simplified case in which u_{1t} and u_{2t} are uncorrelated, (i.e., $\sigma_{12} = 0$) (3.3.6) becomes

$$h(Y_t, p_t) = \frac{|\alpha_1 - \alpha_2|}{2\pi\sigma_1\sigma_2} \exp\left\{-\frac{1}{2}\left[\frac{(Y_t - \alpha_1 p_t - \beta_1' x_{1t})^2}{\sigma_1^2}\right.\right.$$

$$\left.\left. + \frac{(Y_t - \alpha_2 p_t - \beta_2' x_{2t})^2}{\sigma_2^2}\right]\right\}.$$

The product of the densities over all time periods (i.e. observations) for which data are available is the *likelihood function*. *Maximum likelihood estimates* are obtained by maximizing this function (or rather its logarithm) with respect to the unknown parameters α_1, β_1, α_2, β_2, σ_1^2, σ_2^2 and σ_{12} (if present); i.e., declaring that set of parameter values to be our estimates for which the value of

$$L = -T \log 2\pi - \frac{T}{2}\log(\sigma_1^2\sigma_2^2 - \sigma_{12}^2) + T \log|\alpha_1 - \alpha_2|$$

$$- \frac{1}{2(\sigma_1^2\sigma_2^2 - \sigma_{12}^2)} \sum_{t=1}^{T}\left[\sigma_2^2(Y_t - \alpha_1 p_t - \beta_1' x_{1t})^2\right.$$

$$+ \sigma_1^2(Y_t - \alpha_2 p_t - \beta_2' x_{2t})$$

$$\left. - 2\sigma_{12}(Y_t - \alpha_1 p_t - \beta_1' x_{1t})(Y_t - \alpha_2 p_t - \beta_2' x_{2t})\right] \tag{3.3.7}$$

(where T is the total number of observations), is larger than for any other set of parameter values. Parameter estimates obtained in this fashion have the desirable statistical properties of consistency, efficiency and asymptotic normality.

Finding the maximum likelihood estimates is not nearly as routine a computational exercise as, say, computing least squares estimates, since it involves numerical optimization of the function (3.3.7). We comment on this briefly at the end of this section.

The Disequilibrium Model. In the equilibrium model it was taken for granted that all variables, exogenous or endogenous, predetermined or jointly determined, are always observable. This is not the case for the disequilibrium model. This difference is the key to characterizing the econometric distinction between the two approaches and is the source of the difficulties inherent in the disequilibrium model.

In the equilibrium model we assumed that prices are flexible and so adjust as to clear the market. It was this assumption that allowed us to set $D_t = S_t = Y_t$; the "price" we paid for this was that the good's price could not be just any number. In fact, it has to be that unique number that solves (3.3.3) and (3.3.4). In contrast, in the simplest disequilibrium model, we assume that the price does not adjust at all: it is completely rigid. (This assumption is made only for expositional simplicity. In our concrete labor market models the wage is sticky but not completely rigid.) Then D_t need not equal S_t and we are dealing with (3.3.1) and (3.3.2) supplemented by a relation that describes what we observe for quantity, namely

$$Y_t = \min(D_t, S_t). \qquad (3.3.8)$$

This is radically different from the equilibrium approach. In equilibrium we observe Y_t which we know equals both D_t and S_t. Here we observe Y_t and we know that it either equals D_t or S_t, but we do not know which, since D_t and S_t are not observed as such.

Models with some unobservability have become fairly well known. Simple models with some unobservability are the probit and tobit models. (See Chow 1983, chapter 8.) It is interesting to review the statistical issues surrounding probit and tobit models because they share some important traits with disequilibrium models. In the probit model, we posit that a continuous random variable y_t^* is determined from a conventional linear equation,

$$y_t^* = \beta' x_t + u_t,$$

but that y_t^* itself is not observed by the investigator. Instead, she observes a variable y_t which is related to y_t^* by the relations

$$y_t = 1 \text{ if } y_t^* > 0$$

$$y_t = 0 \text{ if otherwise.}$$

In the tobit model the mapping between y_t^* and y_t is somewhat different:

$$y_t = y_t^* \text{ if } y_t^* > 0$$

$$y_t = 0 \text{ otherwise.}$$

Since maximum likelihood estimation has desirable statistical properties, and since the likelihood function is the product over the observations of the densities, it is useful to derive the densities in these models. Consider the probit case. The observable y_t has only two states, 0 and 1, and so we seek the discrete probability distribution of y_t.

By the elementary rules of manipulating probabilities,

$$\Pr\{y_t = 1\} = \Pr\{y_t = 1 | y_t^* > 0\}\Pr\{y_t^* > 0\}$$

$$+ \Pr\{y_t = 1 | y_t^* \leq 0\} \Pr\{y_t^* \leq 0\}$$

and (3.3.9)

$$\Pr\{y_t = 0\} = \Pr\{y_t = 0 | y_t^* > 0\}\Pr\{y_t^* > 0\}$$

$$+ \Pr\{y_t = 0 | y_t^* \leq 0\} \Pr\{y_t^* \leq 0\}$$

where $\Pr\{A | B\}$ denotes the probability of event A *conditional* on event B. But, by definition,

$$\Pr\{y_t = 1 | y_t^* > 0\} = 1$$

$$\Pr\{y_t = 1 | y_t^* \leq 0\} = 0$$

$$\Pr\{y_t = 0 | y_t^* > 0\} = 0$$

$$\Pr\{y_t = 0 | y_t^* \leq 0\} = 1.$$

Thus

$$\Pr\{y_t = 1\} = \Pr\{y_t^* > 0\}$$

$$\Pr\{y_t = 0\} = \Pr\{y_t^* \leq 0\}.$$

If u_t is normally distributed with mean 0 and variance 1.0,[7]

$$\Pr\{y_t^* > 0\} = \Pr\{\beta'x_t + u_t > 0\} = \Pr\{u_t > - \beta'x_t\}$$

$$= 1 - \int_{-\infty}^{t-\beta'x} \frac{1}{\sqrt{2\pi}} e^{-z^2/2} \, dz = \Phi\,(\beta'z_t)$$

where $\Phi(\ )$ denotes the integral of the standard normal density from minus infinity to the indicated argument. As noted above, the likelihood function is the product of the densities and can be written as:

$$L = \prod_{y_t=1} \Phi(\beta'x_t) \prod_{y_t=0} (1 - \Phi(\beta'x_t)). \tag{3.3.10}$$

In the simple disequilibrium model under consideration, life is a bit more complicated but the reasoning is similar. The observable random variable is Y_t, and in analogy with (3.3.9) we can take advantage of basic probability theory to write (Maddala and Nelson 1974, and Quandt 1982):

$$h(Y_t) = f(Y_t|D_t < S_t)\Pr\{D_t < S_t\}$$

$$+ f(Y_t|D_t \geq S_t) \Pr\{D_t \geq S_t\}. \tag{3.3.11}$$

The question is, how do we obtain the conditional density ($f(Y_t|D_t < S_t)$? From (3.3.1) and (3.3.2) we can easily obtain the density $g(D_t,S_t)$ on the assumption (as before) that u_{1t}, u_{2t} are normally distributed with zero means. The conditional density $g(D_t,S_t \mid D_t < S_t)$ is, by the elementary probability rules, $g(D_t,S_t)/\Pr\{D_t < S_t\}$. When the event $D_t < S_t$ occurs, $D_t = Y_t$, so we can write this as $g(Y_t, S_t)/\Pr\{D_t < S_t\}$. The density of Y_t is made up of the densities of all those pairs of D_t ($= Y_t$) and S_t values for which $S_t > D_t$; hence to get all the density of Y_t irrespective of S_t, we must "add up" these individual density values. Since we are dealing with continuous random variables, we must integrate, and thus

$$f(Y_t|D_t < S_t) = \int_{Y_t}^{\infty} g(Y_t,S_t)dS_t/\Pr\{D_t < S_t\}$$

$$f(Y_t|D_t \geq S_t) = \int_{Y_t}^{\infty} g(D_t,Y_t)dD_t/\Pr\{D_t \geq S_t\}.$$

It follows that

$$h(Y_t) = \int_{Y_t}^{\infty} g(Y_t, S_t)dS_t + \int_{Y_t}^{\infty} g(D_t, Y_t)dD_t.$$ (3.3.12)

Working out the algebra for (3.3.12) gives

$$h(Y_t) = \frac{1}{\sqrt{2\pi}\, \sigma_1} \exp\left\{ -\frac{(Y_t - \alpha_1 p_t - \beta_1' x_{1t})^2}{2\sigma_1^2} \right\}$$

$$\times \left[1 - \Phi\left(\frac{(Y_t - \alpha_2 p_t - \beta_2' x_{2t})}{\sigma_2} \right) \right]$$

$$+ \frac{1}{\sqrt{2\pi}\, \sigma_2} \exp\left\{ -\frac{(Y_t - \alpha_2 p_t - \beta_2' x_{2t})^2}{2\sigma_2^2} \right\}$$

$$\times \left[1 - \Phi\left(\frac{(Y_t - \alpha_1 p_t - \beta_1' x_{2t})}{\sigma_1} \right) \right].$$ (3.3.13)

The resulting likelihood function, obtained by multiplying together terms such as (3.3.13) is quite different from and generally more complicated than in the case of the equilibrium model.[8] First of all, the density, and hence the likelihood, contains $\Phi(\ )$, the integral of the normal density, which itself can be computed only as a numerical approximation (although very fast and accurate algorithms exist). More seriously, the resulting likelihood function has a curious property not shared by the equilibrium likelihood; namely, that it can become unbounded in parameter space. What this means is that in the space of potential parameters values there exist some isolated points at which the likelihood function becomes arbitrarily large; yet these points do not normally correspond to reasonable values of the parameters. (For a proof of this see Quandt 1982.) An efficient computational algorithm that is intended to find the maximum of the likelihood function might (and in practice sometimes does) hit upon such points. Although this condition is almost always diagnosed (since it is invariably accompanied by one or the other residual variances becoming zero), and so the investigator is not usually misled into believing that the point arrived at is a reasonable estimate, the condition may sometimes effectively impede the computation of reasonable estimates.

Numerical Optimization. Both equilibrium and disequilibrium likelihood maximization require the use of computer algorithms for numerical optimization. The reason is that the function to be maximized is sufficiently nonlinear, so that as a practical matter the point of maximum value cannot be easily obtained by setting the first partial derivatives equal to zero and solving.

A "simple" algorithm would be to evaluate the likelihood function for all possible combinations of parameter values and choose the combination that leads to the highest value. Such a procedure is not feasible. There are infinitely many parameter combinations that might be considered. Even if one succeeded in restricting one's attention to a finite number, such a procedure would be terribly inefficient— billions of computations would have to be made, outstripping the capacities of even modern computers. Instead, algorithms have been developed which search for an optimum in a more systematic fashion.

Nearly all such algorithms operate by starting at some point in the parameter space, choosing a direction in which the function is improving, taking a (small) step in that direction and then repeating the procedure until some criterion indicates that further function improvements cannot be obtained.

The starting point has to be supplied by the econometrician and immediately suggests that "good guesses," i.e. starting values that happen to be near the ultimate maximum, are very useful. A good direction is obviously one in which the function is increasing relatively most rapidly. In a *local sense,* i.e., for small displacements, the direction of fastest increase is given by the *gradient* of the function, i.e., by the vector that contains as its elements the first partial derivatives of the function. Thus, if the function is $f = -\theta_1^2 - 2\theta_2^2$, which attains its maximum at $\theta_1 = \theta_2 = 0$, the gradient is the vector $(-2\theta_1, -4\theta_2)$; hence, if the initial guess was $\theta_1 = \theta_2 = -1$,

Figure 3.1

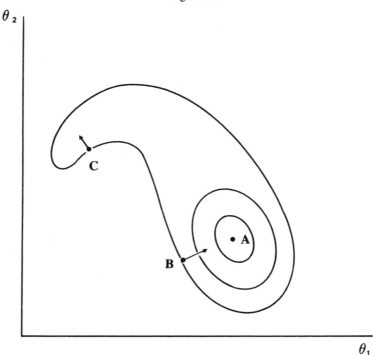

we should take a step that moves two units to the east and four units north.

However, for more complicated functions, this is not an obviously efficient procedure. Consider the function whose contours are depicted in figure 3.1. The maximum is at A. If we happened to start at B, the gradient points approximately in the direction shown by the arrow emanating from B, and obviously carries us roughly in the right direction. But if we happened to start at C, the gradient appears to carry us in the "wrong" direction, at least for a little while. For this reason, more complicated algorithms are often employed; we now briefly outline one of these.

Imagine that the function to be maximized is $F(\theta)$ with θ being an m-parameter vector. Denote by θ^k the value of θ at the kth iteration of the algorithm. Expanding $F(\theta^k)$ in Taylor Series about θ^{k-1}, we could write to an approximation

$$F(\theta^k) = F(\theta^{k-1}) + G(\theta^{k-1})'(\theta^k - \theta^{k-1}) + \frac{1}{2}(\theta^k - \theta^{k-1})'$$
$$H(\theta^{k-1})(\theta^k - \theta^{k-1})$$

where $G(\theta^{k-1})$ is the gradient, i.e., the vector of first partial derivatives and $H(\theta^{k-1})$ is the Hessian, i.e., the matrix of second partial derivatives. To obtain, for given θ^{k-1}, the value of θ^k that maximizes the improvement in the function $F(\theta^k) - F(\theta^{k-1})$, differentiate with respect to θ^k and set the resulting expression equal to zero, yielding

$$G(\theta^{k-1}) + H(\theta^{k-1})(\theta^k - \theta^{k-1}) = 0$$

or

$$\theta^k = \theta^{k-1} - H^{-1}(\theta^{k-1})G(\theta^{k-1}). \tag{3.3.14}$$

Iterating according to (3.3.14) is known as *Newton's Method;* a fast and accurate procedure that requires that the function be concave (otherwise (3.3.14) generates a sequence of θ^k going in the "wrong" direction). Newton's method and its variants (e.g., GRADX; see Goldfeld, Quandt, Trotter 1966) are powerful; however, they are expensive to compute because they require computation of second derivatives, (i.e., the H matrix of equation (3.3.14)). Other algorithms such as the Davidon-Fletcher-Powell (DFP) method or the Powell Conjugate Gradient method are somewhat less reliable but they are also less expensive. In general, there is no method that is best in every situation, and in practice it is useful to have numerous optimization algorithms available.[9]

Appendix 3.1

The Role of the Jacobian of the Transformation

This appendix explains intuitively why the Jacobian of the transformation appears in density functions like equation (3.3.6). The rationale for the Jacobian can be most easily illustrated for the univariate case. Consider a random variable x, with density function f(x), plotted in the first quadrant of figure A3.1. Assume that x is related to y via some specified function x = g(y), plotted in the fourth quadrant of the

Figure A3.1

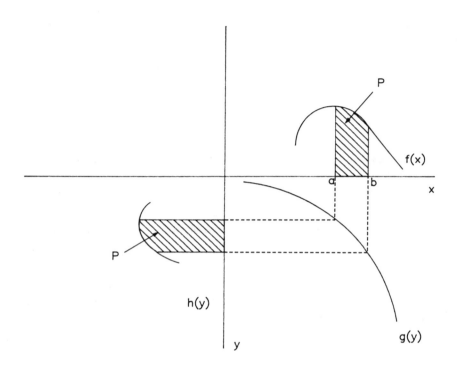

figure. We propose to derive the density of the random variable y.
(Note that if $x = 3y + 4$ and x is random, then y is random). We know
that the resulting density h(y) must have the following property.
Suppose that there is a certain probability, say P, that x is between the
values a and b. Then the probability (calculated from h(y)) that y is
between $g^{-1}(a)$ and $g^{-1}(b)$ must also be P. That means that the shaded
area in the first quadrant, which is approximately f(x)dx (dx is a small
width along the x-axis) must equal the shaded area in the third
quadrant, h(y)dy. But if we substitute g(y) for x and note that by
definition dx $= g'(y)dy$, we have

$$f(x)dx = f(g(y))g'(y)dy = h(y)dy$$

and hence $h(y) = f(g(y))g'(y)$, where $g'(y)$ is the Jacobian of the transformation. Geometrically, if $g(y)$ is steep, a relatively narrow x-interval translates to a relatively wide y-interval; hence to keep shaded areas the same, the height of $h(y)$ must be small. This is just what is accomplished by $g'(y)$, since when $g(y)$ is steep, $dx/dy = g'(y)$ is small.

Appendix 3.2

Derivations of the Disequilibrium Likelihood Function

We derive the disequilibrium model's likelihood function for two cases: (1) errors are uncorrelated over time; and (2) errors in the wage and price equations are serially correlated.

1. *The Basic Model.* For the sake of simplifying the notation, D_t, S_t, w_t, p_t will denote in this appendix the natural logarithm of demand, supply, nominal wage and price, respectively. U_t denotes the measured unemployment rate and z_{1t}, z_{2t}, z_{3t}, z_{4t}, z_{5t} are linear functions of predetermined variables and coefficients. The disequilibrium model can then be written as

$$D_t = \alpha_1 w_t - \alpha_1 p_t + z_{1t} + u_{1t} \tag{A3.1}$$

$$S_t = \beta_1 w_t - \beta_1 p_t + z_{2t} + u_{2t} \tag{A3.2}$$

$$L_t = \min(D_t, S_t) \tag{A3.3}$$

$$w_t = \gamma_2 U_t + \gamma_3 p_t + z_{3t} + u_{3t} \tag{A3.4}$$

$$p_t = \delta_2 w_t + z_{4t} + u_{4t} \tag{A3.5}$$

$$D_t - S_t = \lambda_1/U_t - U_t + z_{5t} + u_{5t} \tag{A3.6}$$

where

$$z_{1t} = \alpha_0 + \alpha_2 \ell n Q_t + \alpha_3 \ell n Q_{t-1} + \alpha_4 t$$

$$z_{2t} = \beta_0 + \beta_1 \ell n(1-\theta_t) + \beta_2 \ell n H_t + \beta_3 \text{ UNION}_t$$

$$z_{3t} = \gamma_0 + \gamma_1 w_{t-1} - \gamma_3 p_{t-1} + \gamma_4(p_{t-1} - p_{t-2}) + \gamma_5 w_{t-2}$$
$$\quad + \gamma_6 \Delta\text{UNION}_t$$

$$z_{4t} = \delta_0 + \delta_1 p_{t-1} - (\delta_2 - \delta_3)w_{t-1} - \delta_3 w_{t-2} + \delta_4(\ell n\ PF_t - \ell nPF_{t-1}) + \delta_5 t$$

$$z_{5t} = 0.$$

Assuming that $u_{1t}, \ldots, u_{5t}$ are jointly normal with mean vector zero and diagonal covariance matrix, the joint probability density function of $(D_t, S_t, w_t, p_t, U_t)$ is

$$f(D_t, S_t, w_t, p_t, U_t) = \frac{|\Delta_t|}{(2\pi)^{5/2}\sigma_1\sigma_2\sigma_3\sigma_4\sigma_5}\ \exp$$

$$\left\{ -\frac{1}{2}\left[\frac{(D_t - \alpha_1 w_t + \alpha_1 p_t - z_{1t})^2}{\sigma_1^2} + \frac{(S_t - \beta_1 w_t + \beta_1 p_t - z_{2t})^2}{\sigma_2^2} \right. \right.$$

$$+ \frac{(w_t - \gamma_2 U_t - \gamma_3 p_t - z_{3t})^2}{\sigma_3^2} + \frac{(p_t - \delta_2 w_t - z_{4t})^2}{\sigma_4^2}$$

$$\left. \left. + \frac{(D_t - S_t - \lambda_1/U_t + U_t - z_{5t})^2}{\sigma_5^2} \right] \right\}, \tag{A3.7}$$

where Δ_t is the Jacobian of the transformation and equals $(\lambda/U_t + 1)(1 - \delta_2\gamma_3) - \alpha_1\gamma_2\delta_2 + \alpha_1\gamma_2 + \beta_1\gamma_2\delta_2 - \beta_1\gamma_2$. The required density is

$$h(L_t, w_t, p_t, U_t) = \int_{L_t}^{\infty} f(D_t, L_t, w_t, p_t, U_t)dD_t$$

$$+ \int_{L_t}^{\infty} f(L_t, S_t, w_t, p_t, U_t)dS_t. \tag{A3.8}$$

Define further

$$z_{6t} = L_t - \lambda_1/U_t + U_t$$

$$z_{7t} = \alpha_1 w_t - \alpha_1 p_t + z_{1t}$$

$$z_{8t} = L_t + \lambda_1/U_t - U_t$$

$$z_{9t} = \beta_1 w_t - \beta_1 p_t + z_{2t}$$

$$\phi_1^2 = \frac{\sigma_2^2 \sigma_5^2}{\sigma_2^2 + \sigma_5^2}$$

$$\phi_2^2 = \frac{\sigma_1^2 \sigma_5^2}{\sigma_1^2 + \sigma_5^2}$$

$$A_t = \frac{\sigma_5^2 z_{9t} + \sigma_2^2 z_{6t}}{\sigma_5^2 + \sigma_2^2} \qquad B_t = \frac{\sigma_5^2 z_{9t}^2 + \sigma_2^2 z_{6t}^2}{\sigma_5^2 + \sigma_2^2}$$

$$C_t = \frac{\sigma_5^2 z_{7t} + \sigma_1^2 z_{8t}}{\sigma_5^2 + \sigma_1^2} \qquad F_t = \frac{\sigma_5^2 z_{7t}^2 + \sigma_1^2 z_{8t}^2}{\sigma_5^2 + \sigma_1^2}.$$

Performing the integrations indicated in (A3.7) yields

$$h(L_t, w_t, p_t, U_t) = G_{1t}(G_{2t} G_{3t} + G_{4t} G_{5t}) \qquad (A3.9)$$

where

$$G_{1t} = \frac{|\Delta_t|}{2\pi\sigma_3\sigma_4} \exp\left\{ -\frac{1}{2}\left[\frac{(w_t - \gamma_2 U_t - \gamma_3 p_t - z_{3t})^2}{\sigma_3^2} \right.\right.$$

$$\left.\left. + \frac{(p_t - \delta_2 w_t - z_{4t})^2}{\sigma_4^2} \right]\right\}$$

$$G_{2t} = \frac{1}{(2\pi)^{1/2}\sigma_1} \exp\left\{ -\frac{1}{2}\left[\frac{(L_t - z_{7t})^2}{\sigma_1^2} \right]\right\}$$

$$G_{3t} = \frac{1}{(2\pi)^{1/2}(\sigma_2^2 + \sigma_5^2)^{1/2}} \exp\left\{ -\frac{1}{2\phi_1^2}(B - A_t^2)\right\}\left[1 - \Phi\left(\frac{L_t - A_t}{\phi_1}\right)\right]$$

$$G_{4t} = \frac{1}{(2\pi)^{1/2}\sigma_2} \exp\left\{-\frac{1}{2}\left[\frac{(L_t-z_{9t})^2}{\sigma_2^2}\right]\right\}$$

$$G_{5t} = \frac{1}{(2\pi)^{1/2}(\sigma_1^2+\sigma_5^2)^{1/2}} \exp\left\{-\frac{1}{2\phi_2^2}(E_t-C_t^2)\right\}\left[1 - \Phi\left(\frac{L_t-C_t}{\phi_2}\right)\right]$$

$$\Phi(\omega) = \int_{-\infty}^{\omega} \frac{1}{\sqrt{2\pi}} e^{-x^2/2}dx.$$

The loglikelihood then is

$$L = \sum_t \log h(L_t,w_t,p_t,U_t). \tag{A3.10}$$

2. *Autocorrelated Error Terms.* We assume that u_{3t} and u_{4t} follow first order Markov processes $u_{3t} = \rho_3 u_{3t-1} + \epsilon_{3t}$, $u_{4t} = \rho_4 u_{4t-1} + \epsilon_{4t}$. Hence, denoting by u_i and ϵ_i the vectors of errors ($i = 3,4$), we can write

$$R_i u_i = \epsilon_i \quad i = 3,4$$

where

$$R_i = \begin{bmatrix} (1-\rho_i^2)^{1/2} & 0 & \cdots & 0 \\ -\rho_i & 1 & \cdots & 0 \\ \cdots\cdots\cdots\cdots\cdots\cdots\cdots\cdots \\ 0 & 0 & -\rho_i & 1 \end{bmatrix}$$

Transforming from the ϵ's to the u's alters only G_{1t}. In analogy with single equation models, the first term is unchanged except for the introduction of $(1-\rho_i^2)^{1/2}$ into the Jacobian and of $(1-\rho_i^2)$ into the matching term of the exponent. In the other terms each squared residual in the exponent is replaced by the square of that residual minus its lagged value which has been multiplied by the matching ρ_i.

NOTES

[1]After a 43-page discussion of macroeconomic theory, Modigliani (1944) observes that the nature of the long-run equilibrium "is not unique since it depends on assumptions concerning the form of the supply-of-labor schedule" (p. 88).

[2]This model is similar in spirit to the one in Quandt and Rosen (1986), but differs in several important respects.

[3]An implicit assumption behind our labor model is that the variable of interest is total hours employed. Thus, workers and hours per worker enter multiplicatively. Feldstein (1967) and Bernanke (1984) have argued that this assumption may be unrealistic. Perhaps, for example, increasing the number of hours by 1 percent does not have the same impact on output as increasing the number of workers by 1 percent. However, the complications involved in dealing with this possibility would take us too far afield from our central focus.

[4]If the underlying production function is assumed to have a constant elasticity of substitution (CES), the coefficients in (3.2.4) can be used to solve the following set of interdependent equations for the CES parameters: $\alpha_1 = -\sigma$, $(\alpha_2 + \alpha_3) = (\sigma h + 1 - \sigma)/h$, and $\alpha_4 = -\lambda (1 - \sigma)/h$, where σ is the elasticity of substitution, h measures returns to scale, and λ is the rate of Hicks-neutral technological change. Although this is an interesting interpretation, the usefulness of (3.2.4) does not rest upon the CES specification. (See remark (ii) in section 3.1.)

[5]We experimented with the more general formulation $\lambda_2/(U_t - \lambda_1) + \lambda_3$, and found that it did not significantly increase the explanatory power of the model.

[6]More precisely, the probability that a given pair will belong to any region of the (u_{1t}, u_{2t}) plane can be found by integrating $f(\cdot)$ over that region.

[7]In the probit model the variance is not separately identifiable and it is customary to normalize it to unity.

[8]Although we do not linger over the individual steps of the derivation, the likelihood function for the principal disequilibrium model of this study is given in appendix 3.2.

[9]For a review of algorithms see Quandt (1983). The present study employed various algorithms in the GQOPT package obtainable from R. E. Quandt.

4

Estimating the Disequilibrium Model

4.1 Restatement of the Model

In this chapter we discuss the data, outline the estimation procedure, and present our results. For purposes of reference we restate the model:

$$\ell nD_t = \alpha_0 + \alpha_1 \ell n\,(W_t/P_t) + \alpha_2 \ell n\,Q_t$$
$$+ \alpha_3 \ell n\,Q_{t-1} + \alpha_4 t + u_{1t} \qquad (4.1.1)$$

$$\ell nS_t = \beta_0 + \beta_1 \ell n\,(W_{nt}/P_t) + \beta_2 \ell n\,H_t$$
$$+ \beta_3 UNION_t + u_{2t} \qquad (4.1.2)$$

$$\ell nL_t = \min(\ell nS_t,\, \ell nD_t) \qquad (4.1.3)$$

$$\ell nW_t = \gamma_0 + \gamma_1 \ell nW_{t-1} + \gamma_2 U_t$$
$$+ \gamma_3\,(\ell nP_t - \ell nP_{t-1})$$
$$+ \gamma_4\,(\ell nP_{t-1} - \ell nP_{t-2}) + \gamma_5 \ell nW_{t-2}$$
$$+ \gamma_6 \Delta UNION_t + u_{3t} \qquad (4.1.4)$$

$$\ell nP_t = \delta_0 + \delta_1 \ell nP_{t-1} + \delta_2(\ell nW_t - \ell nW_{t-1})$$
$$+ \delta_3(\ell nW_{t-1} - \ell nW_{t-2})$$
$$+ \delta_4(\ell nPF_t - \ell nPF_{t-1}) + \delta_5 t + u_{4t} \qquad (4.1.5)$$

$$\ell nD_t - \ell n\,S_t = \frac{\lambda}{U_t} - U_t + u_{5t.} \qquad (4.1.6)$$

All the equations (except (4.1.3)) differ from their counterparts above by the addition of the error terms $u_1, \ldots, u_5$, whose joint distribution is specified below. Appending an error term to the "min condition" is possible in theory, but it leads to a substantial increase in computational costs.

It is routine to establish that the system (minus equation (4.1.3))

43

satisfies the necessary and sufficient conditions for identifiability in a nonlinear system. (See Fisher 1966.)

4.2 *Data*

We describe here briefly the definitions of the variables. The sources and methods of construction are detailed in appendix 4.1, and the numbers presented in the appendix at the end of the book.

The data are annual observations on the U.S. economy for the years 1929 through 1983. L_t is total private hours worked per year expressed in billions. The nominal gross hourly wage measured in dollars, W_t, is formed by dividing total civilian compensation by L_t. Q_t is gross national product measured in billions of 1972 dollars. P_t is the consumer price index, scaled so that the value in 1967 is 100.00. H_t, the potential labor force measured in billions, is constructed by taking the number of people between the ages of 16 and 65, and multiplying by the average number of hours worked per person. The implicit assumption here is that in any given year, those absent from the labor force can potentially contribute an annual number of hours equal to the average of those in the labor force.

The marginal net wage W_{nt}, is the product of the gross wage W_t and a factor $(1 - \theta_t)$, where θ_t is the average marginal federal income tax rate. U_t is the official unemployment rate as a fraction of the labor force. PF_t is the implicit rate deflator for fuel oil and coal. Finally, the unionization rate, $UNION_t$, is union membership as a proportion of the labor force.

4.3 *Stochastic Specification and Estimation Procedure*

We assume that the error terms u_{it} $(i = 1, \ldots, 5)$ are distributed normally with mean zero and diagonal covariance matrix with elements σ_i^2 $(i = 1, \ldots, 5)$ on the main diagonal. We further assume that $E(u_{it}u_{i\tau}) = 0$ for $i = 1, \ldots, 5$ and all t not equal to τ, *except that* the error terms in the nominal wage and price equations are serially correlated according to first order Markov processes with coefficients ρ_1 and ρ_2, respectively. Typically, serial correlation is ignored in disequilibrium models because its presence in equations involving latent variables tends to render the likelihood function intractable. (For special exceptions, see Laffont and Monfort 1979, and Quandt 1982.)

For our case, serial correlation is introduced in the two equations not involving latent variables, which makes the likelihood complicated but not intractable.

The general estimation strategy is as described in section 3.4. A detailed derivation of the likelihood function is in appendix 3.2. The likelihood functions were maximized numerically, using a variety of optimization algorithms, also as described in section 3.4.

4.4 *Parameter Estimates*

The maximum likelihood estimates of the system (4.1.1)–(4.1.6) are presented in column 1 of table 4.1 The numbers in parentheses to the right of the coefficients are their associated t-values, i.e., the coefficients divided by their asymptotic standard errors.

Consider first the demand equation. The value of α_1 implies that the demand elasticity with respect to the real wage is -0.69, an estimate within the range reported by Hamermesh (1984) in his survey of labor demand equations. Similarly, the long run output elasticity (found by adding α_2 and α_4) is about 0.80, a quite reasonable figure. The coefficient on t, α_3, is about 0.0036, suggesting a very mild positive trend in the demand for labor. All coefficients except the one on lagged output are statistically significant at conventional levels.

The supply parameters also appear to be in line with *a priori* notions. The elasticity of labor supply with respect to the after-tax wage, β_1, is about 0.14. Analyses of time series data have consistently found labor supply elasticities that are small in absolute value. The elasticity of labor supply with respect to the potential number of hours, β_2, is 0.67, which is lower than one would expect. Note, however, that adding twice its standard error to β_2 puts it near 0.90. The coefficient on the unionization variable, β_3, is negative, lending support to the hypothesis that unions can reduce the supply of labor. However, the associated t-statistic is only -1.365; we shall have more to say about this shortly.

In the nominal wage adjustment equation, as expected the coefficients on lagged wages (γ_1 and γ_5), and current and lagged prices (γ_3 and γ_4), are positive. The coefficient of U_t, γ_2, is negative, indicating

TABLE 4.1 *Parameter Estimates in the Disequilibrium Model* (t-values in parentheses)

	(1)		(2)	
α_0	−3.056	(−8.679)	−3.056	(−8.487)
α_1	−0.6852	(−20.18)	−0.6852	(−19.77)
α_2	0.7396	(15.76)	0.7396	(12.77)
α_3	0.003587	(2.929)	0.003587	(2.816)
α_4	0.05781	(1.848)	0.05781	(1.124)
β_0	1.995	(2.822)	1.994	(2.036)
β_1	0.1429	(3.873)	0.1429	(2.817)
β_2	0.6697	(6.640)	0.6697	(4.895)
β_3	−0.2918	(−1.365)	−0.2861	(−0.9568)
γ_0	0.2335	(3.917)	0.2313	(3.605)
γ_1	0.3915	(2.883)	0.3883	(2.440)
γ_2	−1.732	(−5.197)	−1.715	(−4.692)
γ_3	0.3801	(2.042)	0.3805	(1.667)
γ_4	0.5976	(3.024)	0.6065	(2.707)
γ_5	0.5493	(4.114)	0.5534	(3.574)
γ_6	−0.002625	(−0.2386)	—	—
δ_0	−0.07249	(−2.491)	−0.07249	(−2.234)
δ_1	0.9575	(22.31)	0.9574	(22.31)
δ_2	0.2509	(3.200)	0.2513	(2.820)
δ_3	0.1721	(2.858)	0.1719	(2.583)
δ_4	0.1712	(3.921)	0.1713	(3.921)
δ_5	0.1905	(4.881)	0.1904	(4.532)
λ	0.001340	(7.130)	0.001340	(7.050)
ρ_1	0.2548	(1.813)	0.2537	(1.441)
ρ_2	0.8850	(10.34)	0.8828	(10.05)
σ_1^2	3.46×10^{-4}	(4.963)	3.46×10^{-4}	(4.961)
σ_2^2	2.58×10^{-3}	(5.101)	2.58×10^{-3}	(5.084)
σ_3^2	1.32×10^{-3}	(3.661)	1.31×10^{-3}	(3.372)
σ_4^2	3.87×10^{-4}	(4.298)	3.87×10^{-4}	(4.121)
σ_5^2	9.03×10^{-7}	(3.499)	9.03×10^{-7}	(3.499)
logL	500.32		500.31	

that a higher official unemployment rate is associated with lower nominal wages and conversely.

The negative value of γ_6 suggests that increases in unionization lead to smaller nominal wages, but the t-statistic is only about −0.24. Taken together with the weak statistical significance of β_3 in the supply equation, this result suggests that the overall impact of unionization on wages and prices is rather weak. Perhaps, however, either of the unionization variables would be more significant if the other were omitted. In column 2 of table 4.1, we show the outcome when the model is estimated with γ_6 set equal to zero. Note that: (i) α_4 and its standard error are essentially unchanged; and (ii) the other parameter estimates change only minimally.[1]

Turning now to the price adjustment equation, we note that lagged price has a coefficient of about 0.96. The values of δ_2 and δ_3 are positive and statistically significant, suggesting that lagged changes in nominal wages have a positive effect on this period's prices. The coefficient on the percentage change in energy prices, δ_4, is also positive and statistically significant, suggesting that even after lagged wages and prices are taken into account, energy prices exert an independent effect on the price level. The coefficient on the time trend, δ_5, is positive and significant.

Finally, we consider the vacancies-unemployment relationship. The only parameter to be estimated here is λ, whose value is about 0.0013. The positive value is expected: When unemployment increases, the vacancy rate decreases. We discuss below whether the magnitude of the estimated λ is sensible.

In summary, the estimates of table 4.1 have at least a surface plausibility. To determine whether or not they are really reasonable requires some evidence on their implications. Such evidence is provided in subsequent sections of this chapter. In the meantime, we have to make a decision on what to do about the unionization variables. Standard statistical criteria suggest that they could be excluded from the model without significantly reducing its explanatory power. Nevertheless, given the important academic and policy controversies that swirl around the role of unions, a case can be made for retaining the union variables, and finding out whether they are *economically* significant in the sense of having a substantial quantitative impact upon the economy. We have chosen the latter strategy; all subsequent results in this chapter are based on the coefficients in column 1 of table 4.1.[2]

4.5 *Discussion of the Results*

In this section we examine some of the implications of the parameter estimates reported in table 4.1. Such an examination aids in determining whether the disequilibrium model provides a useful framework for analyzing the time series data on the U.S. labor market. It also provides a basis for predicting the effects of certain policy variables upon wages, prices, and unemployment.

Dynamics and Stability. A question of some interest is whether prices and wages in the model are locally stable. That is, when there is a small perturbation to the system, do the variables eventually settle down to stable new values, or do the variables grow arbitrarily large or small?

To begin, since equation (4.1.6) is nonlinear in U_t, we expand in Taylor series about an arbitrary value U_0, yielding

$$\ell n D_t - \ell n S_t = (- \frac{\lambda}{U_0^2} - 1) U_t + C_t$$

where C_t has different values for different periods but can be treated as a constant in any one period. Solving for U_t, substituting for D_t and S_t from the demand and supply equations, and then substituting the resulting expression in equations (4.1.4) and (4.1.5), respectively, yields

$$\ell n W_t = \gamma_0 + \gamma_1 \ell n W_{t-1} - \gamma_2 \left[\frac{(\alpha_1 - \beta_1)\ell n W_t - (\alpha_1 - \beta_1)\ell n P_t}{1 + \lambda/U_0^2} \right]$$

$$+ \gamma_3(\ell n P_t - \ell n P_{t-1}) + \gamma_4(\ell n P_{t-1} - \ell n P_{t-2})$$

$$+ \gamma_5 \ell n W_{t-2} + \gamma_6 \, \Delta UNION_t \tag{4.4.1}$$

$$\ell n P_t = \delta_0 + \delta_1 \ell n P_{t-1} + \delta_2(\ell n W_t - \ell n W_{t-1})$$

$$+ \delta_3(\ell n W_{t-1} - \ell n W_{t-2})$$

$$+ \delta_4(\ell n PF_t - \ell n PF_{t-1}) + \delta_5 t. \tag{4.4.2}$$

Stability requires that the roots of the characteristic polynomial for the system (4.4.1), (4.4.2) lie within the unit circle. As we show in appendix 4.2, this condition is satisfied for plausible values of U_0.

Goodness of Fit. How well does the disequilibrium model "explain" the time series data? To explore this question, we computed

Table 4.2 *R²s for the Disequilibrium Model*

ℓnL_t	ℓnP_t	ℓnW_t	U_t
0.945	0 .998	0.998	0.909

for each period the model's prediction for quantity for labor (ℓnL_t), price level (ℓnP_t), nominal wage (ℓnW_t), and official unemployment rate (U_t).[3] For each variable, we regressed the actual on the predicted value each period, and then computed the R^2. The results are recorded in table 4.2. For all variables, the R^2s are high. Of course, this observation does not prove that the model is "right." After all, the current values of ℓnW_t and ℓnP_t depend on their lagged values, and given the high amount of autocorrelation in the data, any macro-economic model with lagged dependent variables is likely to perform well by this criterion. On the other hand, ℓnL_t and U_t are *not* functions of their past values, yet the fit is still pretty good.[4] In short, without making too much of it, we find it comforting that the R^2s are reasonably high.

Excess Demand for Labor and Unemployment Predictions. One of the main reasons for estimating a disequilibrium model of the labor market is to produce estimates of excess demand. The strength of excess demand can be measured in several ways:

(i) ($\ell nD_t - \ell nS_t$). Each period the model generates estimates of the notional demand and supply for labor. Their difference, the percentage excess demand for labor, provides a measure of unemployment that, in theory, is superior to the official measure. For every year we computed the model's reduced form prediction of excess demand as follows: substitute the appropriate values of the exogenous and lagged endogenous variables into equations $(4.1.1) - (4.1.6)$; solve the entire system for the jointly dependent variables; and use the result to calculate $\ell nD_t - \ell nS_t$.[5]

(ii) Simulated Average ($\ell nD_t - \ell nS_t$). Procedure (i) amounts to substituting exogenous and predetermined variables into the various equations. However, in nonlinear systems, the predictions so obtained may be misleading. Therefore, we performed some stochastic simulations. (See Portes, Quandt, Winter and Yeo, 1987.) The simulation

strategy was to solve for the jointly determined variables *after* we added to each structural equation a normal deviate with the same variance as was estimated for that equation. We repeated this procedure 100 times for each time period, and then calculated for each period the average excess demand over the 100 replications.

(iii) $Pr(D_t > S_t \mid L_t)$. Measures (i) and (ii) are essentially point estimates of excess demand. Another issue is whether there was excess demand at all. We therefore compute for each year the probability of excess demand (conditional on the amount of labor).[6]

(iv) Simulated Fraction of Times that $D_t > S_t$. Taking advantage of the procedure outlined in (ii) above, we simulated the model 100 times each period, and found the fraction of times that demand exceeded supply.

In table 4.3 we display the four measures for each year. As expected, the values of all the indicators in 1932–1940 indicate very substantial excess supplies. More generally, all series tell a very similar story qualitatively. Estimated excess demand, $(\ell n D_t - \ell n S_t)$, is negative in all years except 1943–45, 1948, 1952–53, and 1979–80. (Note, however, that for 1979–80 the figures are essentially zero.) In cases where the simulated average excess demand figures differ in sign from $(\ell n D_t - \ell n S_t)$; i.e., in 1946, 1951, 1954, 1956, 1979, and 1980; it is always a very small negative number versus a very small positive number—both measures are really saying that excess demand is about zero. The probabilities of excess demand by the two measures show fairly substantial agreement with the patterns of excess demand and fair agreement with one another. On the whole, the two excess demand measures and the simulated fraction of times that $D_t > S_t$ agree better with one another than any of these agrees with $Pr\{D_t > S_t \mid L_t\}$. A probable reason for this discrepancy is that the latter measure is conditional on the observed L_t whereas the former three are not. This is also the reason why $Pr\{D_t > S_t \mid L_t\}$ exhibits more ones and zeros than the simulated fraction of times that $D_t > S_t$. Since $Pr\{D_t > S_t \mid L_t\}$ uses more information in a sense, it provides a sharper discrimination between periods of excess demand and supply, whereas somewhat more "fuzziness" is observable in the figures on the simulated fraction of times that $D_t > S_t$.

The last column of table 4.3 shows the official unemployment rate

Table 4.3 *Excess Demand Forecasts*

	$\ell nD_t - \ell nS_t$	Simulated Average $\ell nD_t - \ell nS_t$	$Pr(D_t > S_t | L_t)$	Simulated fraction of times that $D_t > S_t$	Official U_t
1932	−0.220	−0.192	0.0	0.0	0.236
1933	−0.240	−0.239	0.0	0.0	0.249
1934	−0.188	−0.214	0.0	0.0	0.217
1935	−0.218	−0.282	0.0	0.0	0.201
1936	−0.176	−0.219	0.0	0.0	0.169
1937	−0.153	−0.177	0.0	0.0	0.143
1938	−0.168	−0.182	0.0	0.0	0.190
1939	−0.163	−0.186	0.0	0.0	0.172
1940	−0.137	−0.152	0.0	0.0	0.146
1941	−0.071	−0.082	0.0	0.01	0.099
1942	−0.001	−0.006	0.0	0.40	0.047
1943	0.151	0.171	0.0	1.00	0.019
1944	0.195	0.231	1.00	1.00	0.012
1945	0.167	0.240	1.00	1.00	0.019
1946	−0.027	0.034	1.00	0.70	0.039
1947	−0.054	−0.011	0.0	0.29	0.039
1948	0.005	0.058	0.0	0.89	0.038
1949	−0.038	−0.012	0.0	0.30	0.059
1950	−0.045	−0.030	0.0	0.18	0.053
1951	−0.002	0.027	0.0	0.68	0.033
1952	0.019	0.062	1.00	0.88	0.030
1953	0.035	0.089	1.00	0.96	0.029
1954	−0.010	0.022	1.00	0.68	0.055
1955	−0.017	−0.006	0.0	0.41	0.044
1956	−0.020	0.019	0.0	0.64	0.041
1957	−0.038	−0.021	0.0	0.25	0.043
1958	−0.059	−0.042	0.0	0.12	0.068
1959	−0.051	−0.040	0.0	0.12	0.055
1960	−0.054	−0.041	0.0	0.11	0.055
1961	−0.061	−0.051	0.0	0.09	0.067
1962	−0.056	−0.045	0.0	0.10	0.055
1963	−0.055	−0.046	0.0	0.08	0.057
1964	−0.056	−0.046	0.0	0.06	0.052
1965	−0.047	−0.041	0.0	0.10	0.045
1966	−0.029	−0.015	0.0	0.30	0.038
1967	−0.025	−0.015	0.0	0.27	0.038
1968	−0.024	−0.007	0.0	0.42	0.036
1969	−0.032	−0.028	0.96	0.17	0.035
1970	−0.045	−0.033	1.0	0.15	0.049
1971	−0.054	−0.049	0.0	0.06	0.059

Table 4.3 *Excess Demand Forecasts, (continued)*

	$\ell nD_t - \ell nS_t$	Simulated Average $\ell nD_t - \ell nS_t$	$Pr(D_t > S_t \vert L_t)$	Simulated fraction of times that $D_t > S_t$	Official U_t
1972	−0.057	−0.056	0.0	0.03	0.056
1973	−0.042	−0.047	0.0	0.05	0.049
1974	−0.030	−0.041	0.0	0.12	0.056
1975	−0.009	−0.011	0.0	0.37	0.085
1976	−0.050	−0.062	0.0	0.03	0.077
1977	−0.037	−0.053	0.0	0.07	0.071
1978	−0.027	−0.042	0.0	0.14	0.061
1979	0.005	−0.003	0.0	0.44	0.058
1980	0.001	−0.005	0.0	0.41	0.071
1981	−0.005	−0.019	0.0	0.29	0.076
1982	−0.034	−0.051	0.0	0.03	0.097
1983	−0.067	−0.099	0.0	0.0	0.096

for each year. There may be a tendency to judge the excess demand figures in the first two columns by how close they correspond to the U_t series in the last column. Although we do expect some similarities in the movements of excess demand and official unemployment, it must be recalled that they are probably measuring quite distinct things. (See the discussion of the vacancies equation in section 3.2 above.) It seems to us that the excess demand figures correspond more closely to the standard theoretical notions of "unemployment" than do the official unemployment rate numbers.

"Phillips Curve". What does our model imply about the short run trade-off between official unemployment and wage inflation? Of course, these two variables are jointly determined, so it does not make sense simply to plug in the value of one and find the implied value of the other. Instead, we consider how both would move under alternative aggregate demand policies. Specifically, the exogenous values of the model except output (Q_t) are set equal to their 1982 values. We then substitute a number of hypothetical values for Q_{1982} into the system, some higher than the actual value in 1982, and some lower. For every value of Q_{1982}, the model is solved to find the associated values of U_{1982} and ($\ell n W_{1982} - \ell nW_{1981}$). This procedure allows us to examine

how wage inflation and unemployment jointly vary under alternative aggregate demand conditions.

The results represent an almost linear relationship characterized by the equation $(\ell n\, W_{1982} - \ell n\, W_{1981}) = 0.187 - 1.84\, U_{1981}$. To attain a nominal wage growth of only 3.5 percent would require an official unemployment rate of 8.3 percent. Alternatively, if the official unemployment rate were 3.5 percent, one would expect nominal wage growth of 12.3 percent. The (approximate) equations for the Phillips curve for other recent years are very similar.

Four points should be made regarding our Phillips Curve experiments:

(i) They say *nothing* about whether monetary or fiscal policy is more effective in bringing about changes in unemployment and inflation. This is because in our model the level of output drives changes in unemployment and inflation, and output is exogenous. Presumably, a discussion of the relative efficacy of monetary and fiscal policies requires a model in which output is endogenous and influenced by government macroeconomic policy. Having said this, we hasten to add that it is still quite interesting from a policy point of view to see how unemployment and inflation will react to changes in output, however the latter is determined.

(ii) The conceptual experiment behind these calculations concerns the short run trade-off between the unemployment rate and the percentage increase in nominal wages. It is now widely agreed that in the long run, the rate of unemployment is independent of the inflation rate. Although we considered imposing this constraint on the model, we ultimately decided that a better strategy would be to let the data determine the coefficients, and to refrain from giving these estimates a long run interpretation.

(iii) Our estimate of -1.84 for the slope coefficient of the Phillips Curve is rather greater in absolute value than typical econometric estimates, which center around -0.4. These "standard" results are obtained by estimating time series regressions. As such, they may be influenced by structural changes in the economy over time. In contrast, our Phillips Curve estimate is formed on the basis of hypothetical changes in aggregate demand within a given year.

(iv) Since we estimate our Phillips Curve by simulating the response to changes in Q_t, a by-product of our calculations is an estimate of the relationship between percentage changes in the real level of output and the rate of unemployment. That is, we can estimate the parameter ζ in the equation $\zeta \, \Delta U_t = \Delta \ell n Q_t$. According to "Okun's Law," $\zeta = -2.5$. Given the nonlinear structure of our model, the value of ζ depends on where U_t and Q_t are evaluated. For low values of U_t (around 0.02), we find $\zeta = -9.29$; for medium values of U_t (around 0.05), $\zeta = -3.70$; and for high values of U_t (around 0.11), $\zeta = -2.57$. Interestingly, then, for high unemployment rates, our estimate matches Okun's. Note also that according to these estimates of ζ, a given percentage increase in aggregate demand has a greater impact on U_t at high levels of unemployment than at low levels. This is consistent with a kind of "diminishing returns" to eliminating unemployment.

"*Natural Rate of Unemployment.*"   Closely related to the Phillips Curve is the "natural rate of unemployment"—the official rate of unemployment that is compatible with constant growth of prices and nominal wages. We impose a constant rate of inflation by requiring $(\ell n P_t - \ell n P_{t-1}) = (\ell n W_t - \ell n W_{t-1}) = G$ in equations (4.1.4) and (4.1.5), where G is a constant.[7] Appendix 4.3 proves that the official rate of unemployment compatible with these conditions, U_t^N, is the positive root of the equation $AU_t^2 + BU_t - \lambda = 0$, where

$$A = 1 + \frac{(\alpha_1 - \beta_1)\gamma_2}{1 - \gamma_1 - \gamma_5};$$

$$B = (\alpha_1 - \beta_1)(\overline{W} - \overline{P}) + z_{1t} - z_{2t};$$

$$\overline{P} = [\delta_0 + G(\delta_2 + \delta_3 - \delta_1) + \delta_4(\ell n PF_t - \ell n PF_{t-1}) + \delta_5 t]/(1 - \delta_1);$$

$$\overline{W} = [\gamma_0 + G(\gamma_3 + \gamma_4 - \gamma_1 - 2\gamma_5)]/(1 - \gamma_1 - \gamma_5). \qquad (4.4.3)$$

In some macroeconomic models, U_t^N is required to be independent of the value of G. That requirement is not imposed here, so we computed U_t^N for two values of G, 0.0 and 0.05. We evaluated (4.4.3) for each year in the sample period and found that when $G = 0.0$, the average value of U_t^N is 13.0 percent, and when $G = 0.05$, its average value is 5.6 percent. The annual values of U_t^N conditional on $G = 0.05$ are reported in the first column of table 4.4. The values of U_t^N in the

Table 4.4 *Natural Unemployment Rates and Vacancy Rates*

Year	Natural Unemployment Rate (G = 0.05)	Vacancy Rate
1932	0.0372	0.00591
1933	0.0627	0.00547
1934	0.0958	0.00687
1935	0.0611	0.00599
1936	0.0721	0.00729
1937	0.0692	0.00832
1938	0.0625	0.00761
1939	0.0573	0.00783
1940	0.0719	0.00914
1941	0.0719	0.0155
1942	0.0764	0.0360
1943	0.0626	0.160
1944	0.0485	0.202
1945	0.0381	0.175
1946	0.0669	0.0254
1947	0.0944	0.0184
1948	0.103	0.0392
1949	0.0465	0.0222
1950	0.0532	0.0205
1951	0.0537	0.0357
1952	0.0427	0.0472
1953	0.0467	0.0578
1954	0.0373	0.0321
1955	0.0391	0.0289
1956	0.0467	0.0279
1957	0.0525	0.0223
1958	0.0289	0.0176
1959	0.0379	0.0192
1960	0.0247	0.0184
1961	0.0463	0.0171
1962	0.0301	0.0181
1963	0.0364	0.0183
1964	0.0194	0.0181
1965	0.0342	0.0201
1966	0.0344	0.0247
1967	0.0348	0.0261
1968	0.0337	0.0266
1969	0.0299	0.0238
1970	0.0356	0.0205
1971	0.0440	0.0184
1972	0.0225	0.0180
1973	0.0714	0.0212

Table 4.4 *Natural Unemployment Rates and Vacancy Rates (continued)*

Year	Natural Unemployment Rate $(G = 0.05)$	Vacancy Rate
1974	0.198	0.0246
1975	0.0459	0.0325
1976	0.0449	0.0194
1977	0.0635	0.0226
1978	0.0350	0.0254
1979	0.130	0.0394
1980	0.141	0.0372
1981	0.0906	0.0344
1982	0.143	0.0234
1983	0.00417	0.0162

table exhibit substantial year-to-year variability (from a high of 19.8 percent in 1974 to 0.42 percent in 1983). There appears to be some tendency for declining values of U_t^N from the Great Depression through 1974. After 1974, the values fluctuate somewhat erratically.

A related question is what level of official unemployment would be associated with "true" zero excess demand in the labor market— $(D_t - S_t) = 0$. To compute this figure, we simply note from equation (4.1.6) that when $D_t = S_t$, $\lambda/U_t - U_t = 0$, and find the U_t that satisfies this relationship. According to this calculation, when official unemployment is about 3.7 percent, the labor market is actually in equilibrium.

Vacancy Rates. Recall equation (3.2.11), the relationship between the unobserved vacancy rate (V_t), the observed official unemployment rate (U_t), and the parameter $\lambda : V_t = \lambda/U_t$. Another indicator of the plausibility of our model is whether the magnitudes of the implied values of the vacancy rate are reasonable. To investigate this issue, note from equation (4.1.6) that vacancies are equal to excess demand plus the official unemployment rate. We can therefore substitute our estimates of D_t, S_t and U_t into (4.1.6) to calculate V_t.[8] Given the simple inverse relationship posited between U_t and V_t, we know that V_t will be *relatively* low during the depression, high during World War II, etc. What is reassuring about the results in the second column of Table 4.4 is that the *absolute* magnitudes seem quite reasonable, something that is not guaranteed by the mere fact that $\lambda > 0$.

Table 4.5 *Impact of Changing the Unionization Rate*

Unionization rate	$\ell n\hat{D} - \ell n\hat{S}$	$\hat{U}$	$\Delta\ell n\hat{W}$	$\Delta\ell n\hat{P}$
0.268	−0.018	0.046	0.057	0.047
0.218	−0.026	0.052	0.046	0.045
0.168	−0.033	0.057	0.036	0.042
0.118	−0.042	0.063	0.025	0.039
0.068	−0.049	0.069	0.014	0.036

Specifically, from 1932 to 1940, the estimated vacancy rate is less than 1 percent, during 1943–45 it rises as high as 20 percent, and varies between 1.6 and 5.8 percent thereafter.

Impact of Unionization. As noted earlier, the unionization variables in our model are not significant according to standard statistical criteria. Nevertheless, given the importance that unionization has in debates over public policy, we thought that it would be useful to investigate the quantitative significance of the unionization variables. To do so, we performed two sets of simulations:

(i) We computed for 1982 the model's predictions for excess demand ($\ell n\hat{D} - \ell n\hat{S}$), official unemployment ($\hat{U}$), nominal wage inflation ($\Delta\ell n\hat{W}$) and price level growth ($\Delta\ell n\hat{P}$) under several hypothetical values of the unionization rate.[9] (The actual rate in 1982 was 16.8 percent.) The results are summarized in table 4.5. The main message conveyed by the table is that unionization simply does not have much of a quantitative impact on key macroeconomic variables. For example, a massive change in the unionization rate, from about 12 to 22 percent, would have just slightly more than a 1 percentage point effect on the official employment rate. Curiously, to the extent there is an effect of increasing unionization, it is to *reduce* both excess supply and the official unemployment rate. To understand this counter-intuitive result, recall that in the notional labor supply equation (4.1.2), when $UNION_t$ increases, the supply curve shifts inward, tending to reduce the gap between quantity demanded and quantity supplied at any given wage, i.e., *decreasing* the excess supply of labor. (This effect is reinforced by the negative coefficient on the change in unionism in equation (4.1.4), but that coefficient is very small.) Again, however, we must stress that this phenomenon is quantitatively small.

Table 4.6 *Phillips Curves With Alternative Unionization Rates*

Unionization rate	Intercept	Slope
0.268	0.188	−1.85
0.218	0.187	−1.85
0.168	0.187	−1.84
0.118	0.186	−1.83
0.068	0.185	−1.82

(ii) Using the method described above, we computed Phillips Curves for 1982 under several hypothetical values of the unionization rate. The idea here is to see how unions affect the *trade-off* between unemployment and inflation—does unionization confront policy-makers with a less attractive "menu" of options than would otherwise be the case. The intercept and slope of the Phillips Curve for each unionization rate are presented in table 4.6. They suggest that changing rates of unionization have only imperceptible effects on the short-run inflation-unemployment trade-off.

Impact of Income Taxes. Another important issue in current policy debates is the impact of taxes—how do they affect labor supply, unemployment, wages, etc. In our model, the federal personal income tax rate directly influences the supply of labor, equation (4.1.2), because labor supplied depends upon the net wage. To assess the immediate impact of changing tax policy, we computed for a variety of tax rates the model's predictions for excess demand ($\ell n \hat{D}_t - \ell n \hat{S}_t$), official unemployment ($\hat{U}$), and the rates of wage inflation ($\Delta \ell n \hat{W}$) and price inflation ($\Delta \ell n \hat{P}$). Before considering the results of this experiment, it is important to note again that these calculations are done conditional on the actual level of output. Thus, they have nothing to say about whether tax policy is a successful way of influencing the labor market via aggregate demand.

With this caveat in mind, consider the results reported in table 4.7. The various values of the average marginal tax rate, θ, are in the first column. (The actual value in 1982 was 0.204.) Reading down the column headed $\ell n \hat{D} - \ell n \hat{S}$, we see that excess supply falls as the tax rate increases. Intuitively, this makes sense, because an increase in the tax rate in effect shifts the supply curve in, reducing the discrepancy between quantity demanded and quantity supplied, *ceteris paribus*. From the column headed $\hat{U}$, we see that official unemployment rates also fall as the tax rate increases.

The tax-induced inward shift of the supply curve also increases the before tax wage, as indicated by the column headed $\Delta \ell n \hat{W}_t$. And from the last column, increases in the wage generate increases in prices. Note that the changes in prices induced by tax changes turn out to be relatively small compared to the other changes in the table.

4.6 *Summary*

We have estimated the disequilibrium model consisting of equations (4.1.1) through (4.1.6) using annual data on the U.S. economy for the years 1929 through 1983. For the most part, the parameters seem quite reasonable. The variables in the supply and demand equations have coefficients that are in line with *a priori* notions and that are consistent with many earlier studies. While it is more difficult to say whether the coefficients in the other equations are reasonable, the following observations speak in their behalf: (i) the excess demand predictions generated by the system as a whole are convincing (strong negative excess demand in the depression, positive excess demand during World War II, and generally negative or slightly positive excess demand thereafter); and (ii) the system exhibits local stability, in the sense that when there is a small disturbance, the endogenous variables settle down to stable new values.

The parameter estimates have a number of implications. Three of the most striking are:

(i) There is a substantial short run trade-off between the unemployment rate and the rate of wage inflation. Changes in aggregate demand policy that would increase the proportion of the labor force that is unemployed by 1 percentage point would, in the short run, reduce the rate of wage growth by 1.84 percentage points.

(ii) Changes in unionization exert little discernible impact on the magnitude of wages, prices, unemployment, etc.

(iii) Conditional on the level of aggregate demand, changes in the income tax rate similarly have little short-run effect on key macro-

Table 4.7   *Impact of Changing the Marginal Income Tax Rate*

θ	$\ell n\hat{D}-\ell n\hat{S}$	$\hat{U}$	$\Delta\ell n\hat{W}$	$\Delta\ell n\hat{P}$
0.143	−0.039	0.061	0.028	0.040
0.170	−0.037	0.060	0.032	0.041
0.204	−0.034	0.057	0.036	0.042
0.238	−0.031	0.055	0.041	0.043
0.271	−0.027	0.052	0.045	0.044

economic variables. This is largely a consequence of the small coefficient on the net wage in the labor supply equation.

Of course, as emphasized in chapters 1 and 2, our models are far from the point where they should be used as the basis for formulating economic policy. Nevertheless, the results are plausible, interesting, and demonstrate the potential of disequilibrium models as analytical tools.

Appendix 4.1

Data

This appendix describes the sources and methods of construction of the variables in the model. Throughout, we abbreviate *"National Income and Product Accounts of the United States"* as *N.I.P.A.*

H_t, *the potential labor force in billions of hours,* is the number of civilians between the ages of 16 and 65 multiplied by the average number of hours worked per person. The number of civilians in this age group is calculated by taking the total population between 16 and 65 and subtracting membership in the armed forces (*Economic Report of the President 1984,* pp. 253, 254).

L_t, *total civilian hours worked per year expressed in billions,* is total hours minus hours worked in the military. For 1948–79, the following procedure is used. To find hours worked in the military, compute the ratio of the number of military workers to the total number of government workers (*N.I.P.A. 1929–1976,* pp. 267–69 and *N.I.P.A. 1976–1979,* p. 55) and multiply by the number of hours worked by government employees (*N.I.P.A. 1929–1976,* p. 271 and *N.I.P.A. 1976–1979,* p. 56). This gives hours worked in the military, which is then subtracted from total hours *(N.I.P.A. 1929–1976,* p. 271 and *N.I.P.A. 1976–1979,* p. 55).

For 1929–47, comparable data do not exist. Using a slightly different method, we constructed in Rosen and Quandt (1978) a series on civilian hours extending back to 1929. To splice the two series together, for the period 1948 to 1973 we estimated a regression of the logarithm of civilian hours as calculated above on a time trend and on the logarithm of the Rosen-Quandt measure. The R^2 was 0.992. We then substituted values for the Rosen-Quandt measure from 1929–1947 into the regression equation, and used the fitted values. For 1980–83, a similar splicing procedure was used. Here we regressed the *N.I.P.A.* series on data from a comparable series from the *Economic Report of the President 1984.*

PF_t, *price deflator for fuel and coal,* is from various editions of the *N.I.P.A.*

P_t, *the consumer price index,* is from *Historical Statistics of the United States,* pp. 210–11 for years prior to 1970; and from *Economic Report of the President 1984,* p. 279, for years after 1970. $P_{1967} = 100.0$.

Q_t, *gross national product in 1972 prices,* is from the *Economic Report of the President 1982,* p. 234, for 1941 through 1979 and from *U.S. Department of Commerce, Survey of Current Business,* July 1983, p. 69, for 1980 through 1983.

r_t, *nominal interest rate,*[10] is the yield on Moody's corporate Aaa bonds. For years up to 1970 the source is *Historical Statistics of the United States,* p. 1003, for subsequent years it is *Economic Report of the President 1984,* Table B-67.

$UNION_t$, *union membership as a proportion of the total labor force,* is from *Handbook of Labor Statistics,* December 1980, p. 412 and Gifford (1982).

U_t, *unemployment as a percentage of the civilian labor force,* is from *Historical Statistics of the United States,* p. 135 for 1929–47, and from *Economic Report of the President 1982,* p. 271 for 1948–1981, and *Economic Report of the President 1984,* p. 259 for 1982–83.

W_t, *gross hourly nominal wage measured in dollars,* is the ratio of total civilian compensation to civilian hours worked. Total civilian compensation is total compensation of employees *(N.I.P.A., 1929–1976*, pp. 238–42 and *N.I.P.A. 1976–1979*, p. 52) minus compensation of military employees *(Historical Statistics of the United States*, p. 235; *N.I.P.A. 1929–1976*, pp. 240–42; and *N.I.P.A. 1976–1979*, p. 52). The computation of civilian hours worked is described above. Comparable data do not exist for 1980–83, but there is a CITIBASE series on average hourly compensation for employees in the nonfarm business sector. We spliced our series with the CITIBASE series by means of an ordinary least squares regression of the logarithm of our wage series on the logarithm of the CITIBASE series and a time trend. The regression was estimated over the period 1947–79.

θ_t, *the average marginal tax rate*, is taken from Barro and Sahasakul (1983, p. 20) for years up to and including 1980. For 1981–83, we splice together Barro and Sahasakul's figures with those of Clotfelter (1984).

Appendix 4.2

Dynamics in the Disequilibrium Model

Let E be the forward operator such that $Ex_t = x_{t+1}$. Denote the characteristic matrix for system (4.4.1), (4.4.2) by M. Then the elements of M are defined as follows:

$$M_{11} = \frac{(1+\gamma_2(\alpha_1-\beta_1))}{1 + \lambda/U_0^2} E^2 + \left[-\gamma_1 - \frac{\lambda_2\beta_3}{1 + \lambda/U_0^2} \right] E - \gamma_5$$

$$M_{12} = \left(-\gamma_3 - \frac{\gamma_2(\alpha_1-\beta_1)}{1 + \lambda/U_0^2} \right) E^2 + \left[\frac{\gamma_2\beta_3}{1 + \lambda/U_0^2} + \gamma_3 - \gamma_4 \right] E + \gamma_4$$

$$M_{21} = -\delta_2 E^2 + (\delta_2-\delta_3)E + \delta_3$$

$$M_{22} = E^2 - \delta_1 E.$$

The characteristic polynomial is found by taking the determinant of the matrix M. The polynomial's roots depend on the assumed value U_0 about which the expansion is taken. They were computed for $U_0 = 0.01, 0.02, \ldots , 0.14$. For all of these cases there are three positive roots, one negative root and two complex roots. The maximal modulus decreases monotonically from 0.8340 for $U_0 = 0.01$ to 0.4785 for $U_0 = 0.14$. The system is thus locally stable for all plausible unemployment rates.

Appendix 4.3

Computation of the Natural Rate of Unemployment

We define the natural rate of unemployment to be that rate that is compatible with a constant rate of price and wage inflation. Let this rate be G; then by definition

$$
\begin{aligned}
w_t - w_{t-1} &= G \\
p_t - p_{t-1} &= G
\end{aligned}
\tag{A4.3.1}
$$

for all t, where wages and prices are measured in natural logarithms. It follows from (A4.3.1) that the wage and price adjustment equations (4.1.4), (4.1.5), can be written as

$$
\begin{aligned}
w_t &= \gamma_0 + \gamma_1(w_t - G) + \gamma_2 U_t + \gamma_3 G + \gamma_4 G \\
&\quad + \gamma_5(w_t - 2G) + \gamma_6 \Delta UNION_t \\
p_t &= \delta_0 + \delta_1(p_t - G) + \delta_2 G + \delta_3 G \\
&\quad + \delta_4(\ell nPF_t - \ell nPF_{t-1}) + \delta_5 t,
\end{aligned}
\tag{A4.3.2}
$$

where we suppress the error terms and thus consider a certainty-equivalent solution.

Solving the two equations in (A4.3.2) yields

$$
w_t = \frac{\gamma_0 + G(\gamma_3 + \gamma_4 - \gamma_1 - 2\gamma_5)}{1 - \gamma_1 - \gamma_5} + \frac{\gamma_2 U_t + \gamma_6 \Delta UNION_t}{1 - \gamma_1 - \gamma_5}
$$

$$
\tag{A4.3.3}
$$

$$
p_t = \frac{\delta_0 + G(\delta_2 + \delta_3 - \delta_1) + \delta_4 (\ell nPF_t - \ell nPF_{t-1}) + \delta_5 t}{1 - \delta_1} \equiv \bar{p}_t.
$$

The demand and supply functions (4.1.1), (4.1.2) can be written in abbreviated form as

$$D_t = \alpha_1 w_t - \alpha_1 p_t + z_{1t}$$
$$S_t = \beta_1 w_t - \beta_1 p_t + z_{2t} \tag{A4.3.4}$$

where we again suppress the error terms and where z_{1t}, z_{2t} are functions of coefficients and predetermined variables. For simplicity, define the first term in the first equation of (A4.3.3) as $\bar{w}$; i.e., $\bar{w} = [\gamma_0 + G(\gamma_3 + \gamma_4 - \gamma_1 - 2\gamma_5)]/(1 - \gamma_1 - \gamma_5)$. Combining (A4.3.4) with the vacancy equation (4.1.6) yields

$$(\alpha_1 - \beta_1)\, w_t - (\alpha_1 - \beta_1)\, p_t + z_{1t} - z_{2t} = \frac{\lambda}{U_t} - U_t. \tag{A4.3.5}$$

Substituting (A4.3.3) into (A4.3.5) and multiplying through by U_t gives the quadratic equation

$$AU_t^2 + B_t U_t - \lambda = 0 \tag{A4.3.6}$$

where

$$A = 1 + \frac{(\alpha_1 - \beta_1)\gamma_2}{1 - \gamma_1 - \gamma_5}$$

$$B_t = (\alpha_1 - \beta_1)(\bar{w} - \bar{p}_t) + z_{1t} - z_{2t}.$$

Since A and λ are positive, there can be only one positive root, which is the natural rate of unemployment.

NOTES

[1]Moreover, the coefficients do not change very much when unionization variables are excluded entirely from the model. See Quandt and Rosen (1986).

[2]However, the outcomes do not change substantively when the column 2 parameter values are used instead.

[3]This was done by substituting the appropriate values of the exogenous and predetermined variables into (4.1.1) – (4.1.6), and solving for the endogenous

variables. The value of L_t was the minimum of the S_t and D_t so generated. To solve for U_t we: (i) solve for D_t, S_t, W_t, P_t in terms of U_t; (ii) substitute the results for D_t and S_t in the unemployment-vacancies relation, and then (iii) solve the resulting quadratic for U_t.

[4]For L_t and U_t simple second order regressions lead to about the same R^2s as those reported in table 4.2. When L_t is regressed on first and second order lags $R^2 = 0.965$, which is higher than its counterpart in table 4.2; for U_t the corresponding figure is 0.905, which is lower.

[5]An alternative procedure is to compute $E(\ell nD_t - \ell nS_t | \ell nL_t)$. This is likely to be more efficient than using simply $(\ell n\hat{D}_t - \ell n\hat{S}_t)$ (Goldfeld and Quandt 1981), but is somewhat complicated to compute in the present model and will not be pursued here.

[6]$\Pr\{D_t > S_t | L_t\}$ is computed as the ratio $G_{4t} G_{5t}/(G_{2t} G_{3t} + G_{4t} G_{5t})$, where the G_t's are defined in appendix 3.2. One can also compute the unconditional probability that D_t exceeds S_t. This can be obtained from the reduced form as follows. Let $D_t = H_{1t} + v_{1t}$, $S_t = H_{2t} + v_{2t}$, where H_{1t}, H_{2t} depend only on parameters and coefficients and v_{1t}, v_{2t} are reduced form errors. Then the required probability is $\Pr\{H_{1t} - H_{2t} > v_{2t} - v_{1t}\}$ which can be computed once estimated parameter values are substituted. However, in some applications the probabilities have been found to be very close to the conditional probabilities. (See Burkett 1981.)

[7]Under this assumption, it follows from equation (4.1.4) that U_t will generally depend on both the level of the wage *and* the rate of inflation. However, if $\gamma_1 + \gamma_5 = 1$, then U depends only on G, a much more plausible result. Note from table 4.1 that the sum does appear to be quite close to unity.

[8]When we substitute actual rather than estimated values of the official unemployment rate, qualitatively similar results emerge.

[9]Throughout, we use $\ell n\hat{X}$ to denote the prediction of the natural logarithm of X rather than the logarithm of the prediction of X.

[10]The interest rate appears in the equilibrium model of chapter 5.

5

The Equilibrium Model

In this chapter, we specify and estimate an equilibrium model of the labor market, and discuss its implications.

5.1 *The Basic Structure*

The equilibrium analysis is based on Lucas and Rapping's (L-R) work. However, their model is modified in order to facilitate comparisons with the disequilibrium results of chapter 4. We now discuss the labor demand, labor supply, unemployment and price equations in turn.

Labor Demand. Like our equation (4.1.1), the L-R labor demand equation is a marginal productivity condition that emerges from the firm's cost minimization problem. The only serious difference is that L-R include the lagged quantity of labor on the right hand side:

$$\ell nD_t = \alpha_0 + \alpha_1 \ell n(W_t/P_t) + \alpha_2 \ell nQ_t + \alpha_3 t +$$

$$\alpha_4 \ell nQ_{t-1} + \alpha_5 \ell nL_{t-1} + u_{lt}. \qquad (5.1.1)$$

Lagged labor is present to allow for the possibility of sluggish adjustment to output changes. The time trend is intended to capture technological change.

Labor Supply. A central feature of the equilibrium model is inter-temporal labor supply substitution. Workers' labor supply in period t is based not only on the current real net wage, (W_{nt}/P_t), but also on the expectation of the future net wage formed in period t, $(W_n/P_t)^*$. (In general, we will denote expected values by an asterisk *.) L-R do not correct wages in the supply equation for the presence of taxes; in contrast, we assume that the net wage is relevant for labor supply decisions. The higher the expected future wage, *ceteris*

67

paribus, the less workers should choose to supply in the current period. Hence, if the hypothesis of intertemporal labor supply substitution is correct, $(W_n/P)_t^*$ should have a negative coefficient.

Similarly, with intertemporal substitution, the real interest rate should have an impact on current labor supply decisions. The higher the real interest rate, the greater the future value of money earned in the present, and hence the greater inducement to work in the present. The real interest rate is defined as the nominal interest rate r_t, minus the expected rate of inflation $(\ln P_t^* - \ln P_t)$, where P_t^* is the expectation of the future price level formed in period t. In short, intertemporal labor supply substitution implies that the variable $[r_t - (\ln P_t^* - \ln P_t)]$ will have a positive coefficient in the labor supply equation.

We can summarize this discussion by writing[1]

$$\ln S_t = \beta_0 + \beta_1 \ln(W_{nt}/P_t) - \beta_2 \ln(W_n/P)_t^*$$
$$+ \beta_3[r_t - (\ln P_t^* - \ln P_t)]$$
$$+ \beta_4 \ln H_t + u_{2t}, \qquad (5.1.2)$$

where H_t is the same scale variable used in the disequilibrium model.[2] As in (4.1.2), we augment (5.1.2) with a variable representing the proportion of the workforce that is unionized. Also, we introduce some simple dynamics by entering the lagged net wage, (W_{nt-1}/P_{t-1}). Hence, we have

$$\ln S_t = \beta_0 + \beta_1 \ln(W_{nt}/P_t) - \beta_2 \ln(W_n/P)_t^*$$
$$+ \beta_3[r_t - (\ln P_t^* - \ln P_t)] + \beta_4 \ln H_t$$
$$+ \beta_5 \text{UNION}_t + \beta_6 \ln(W_{nt-1}/P_{t-1})$$
$$+ u_{2t}. \qquad (5.1.3)$$

Observed Quantity of Labor. In the equilibrium model, the observed quantity of labor, L_t, is always at the intersection of supply and demand. Therefore

$$L_t = D_t = S_t. \qquad (5.1.4)$$

Unemployment Rate. In the L-R model, unemployment occurs when the current wage rate is less than the perceived "normal" wage rate. The underlying notion is that the labor force, as measured by the government's Current Population Survey, consists of those who are employed plus those who are unemployed *but* would accept work at their normal wage. Hence, all unemployment is voluntary.

Define $\tilde{L}_t$ as the labor supply at the normal net real wage and the normal price level. L-R argue that it is natural to define the net real wage in period t as being normal if its value is exactly what was predicted last period. Algebraically, (W_{nt}/P_t) is the normal net wage if it equals $(W_n/P)^*_{t-1}$. Similarly, a normal price level is defined by $P_t = P^*_{t-1}$. Substituting these definitions into (5.1.3) (and recalling that $S_t = L_t$), yields

$$\ell n \tilde{L}_t = \beta_0 + \beta_1 \ell n(W_n/P)^*_{t-1} - \beta_2 \ell n(W_n/P)^*_t$$
$$+ \beta_3[r_t - (\ell n P^*_t - \ell n P^*_{t-1})] + \beta_4 \ell n H_t$$
$$+ \beta_5 UNION_t + \beta_6 \ell n(W_n/P)^*_{t-2}$$
$$+ u_{2t}. \qquad (5.1.5)$$

Next subtract (5.1.3) from (5.1.5):

$$\ell n \tilde{L}_t - \ell n L_t = \beta_1\{\ell n (W_n/P)^*_{t-1} - \ell n(W_{nt}/P_t)\}$$
$$+ \beta_3(\ell n P^*_{t-1} - \ell n P_t)$$
$$+ \beta_6\{\ell n(W_n/P)^*_{t-2} - \ell n(W_{nt-1}/P_{t-1})\}$$
$$(5.1.6)$$

Now observe that $\ell n \tilde{L}_t - \ell n L_t$ is approximately the percentage difference between normal employment and actual employment. Thus, it is the rate of unemployment due to intertemporal labor supply substitution.

L-R continue their derivation of the unemployment equation by arguing that the unemployment rate is not exactly equal to $(\ell n \tilde{L}_t - \ell n L_t)$ because of sources of unemployment other than intertemporal substitution, e.g., frictional unemployment. L-R posit that the official unemployment rate, U_t, and $(\ell n \tilde{L}_t - \ell n L_t)$ are related linearly:

$$U_t = g_0 + g_1(\ell n \tilde{L}_t - \ell n L_t). \qquad (5.1.7)$$

Substituting (5.1.6) into (5.1.7) and appending an error term gives us

$$U_t = g_0 + g_1\beta_1\{\ell n(W_n/P)^*_{t-1} - \ell n(W_{nt}/P_t)\}$$
$$+ \beta_3 g_1(\ell n P^*_{t-1} - \ell n P_t) + g_1\beta_6\{\ell n(W_n/P)^*_{t-2}$$
$$- \ell n(W_{nt-1}/P_{t-1})\} + u_{3t}. \tag{5.1.8}$$

Equation (5.1.8) differs from the unemployment equation estimated by L-R only by the presence of the variable multiplying $g_1\beta_6$, which is present because lagged wages are included in our supply equation but not in L-R's. In order to allow for the possibility that increases in the unionization rate[3] may affect unemployment, we augment equation (5.1.8) with the variable $\Delta UNION_t = UNION_t - UNION_{t-1}$:

$$U_t = g_0 + g_1\beta_1\{\ell n(W_n/P)^*_{t-1} - \ell n(W_{nt}/P_t)\}$$
$$+ \beta_3 g_1(\ell n P^*_{t-1} - \ell n P_t) + g_1\beta_6\{\ell n(W_n/P)^*_{t-2}$$
$$- \ell n(W_{nt}/P_{t-1})\} + g_2\Delta UNION_t + u_{3t}. \tag{5.1.9}$$

Note that in a steady state, all variables are at their normal values, and $\Delta UNION$ is zero. Hence, in a steady state U_t is simply equal to g_0, which is purely frictional unemployment and can be interpreted as the model's natural rate of unemployment. In other words, the long run Phillips Curve is vertical at an unemployment rate of g_0.

Prices. In the Lucas-Rapping model, the price level is exogenous. Given that the disequilibrium model of chapter 4 has a price equation, it seemed to us that simply taking P_t as predetermined would handicap the equilibrium model in any comparisons. We therefore include a price equation similar to (4.1.5):

$$\ell n P_t = \delta_0 + \delta_1 \ell n P_{t-1} + \delta_2(\ell n W_t - \ell n W_{t-1})$$
$$+ \delta_3(\ell n W_{t-1} - \ell n W_{t-2})$$
$$+ \delta_4(\ell n PF_t - \ell n PF_{t-1}) + u_{4t}, \tag{5.1.10}$$

where, as before, PF_t refers to fuel prices. We estimated a version of (5.1.10) including a time trend (as in equation (4.1.5)), but its addition virtually had no effect on the loglikelihood value.

5.2 Modeling Expectations

At this point it is useful to summarize the basic equilibrium model:

$$\ell nD_t = \alpha_0 + \alpha_1 \ell n(W_t/P_t) + \alpha_2 \ell nQ_t + \alpha_3 t$$
$$+ \alpha_4 \ell nQ_{t-1} + \alpha_5 \ell nL_{t-1} + u_{1t} \qquad (5.2.1)$$

$$\ell nS_t = \beta_0 + \beta_1 \ell n(W_{nt}/P_t) - \beta_2 \ell n(W_n/P)_t^* + \beta_3[r_t$$
$$- (\ell nP_t^* - \ell nP_t)] + \beta_4 \ell nH_t + \beta_5 UNION_t$$
$$+ \beta_6 \ell n(W_{nt-1}/P_{t-1}) + u_{2t} \qquad (5.2.2)$$

$$L_t = S_t = D_t \qquad (5.2.3)$$

$$U_t = g_0 + g_1\beta_1\{\ell n(W_n/P)_{t-1}^* - \ell n(W_{nt}/P_t)\}$$
$$+ \beta_3 g_1(\ell nP_{t-1}^* - \ell nP_t) + g_1\beta_6\{\ell n(W_n/P)_{t-1}^*$$
$$- \ell n(W_{nt-1}/P_{t-1})\} + g_2\Delta UNION_t + u_{3t} \qquad (5.2.4)$$

$$\ell nP_t = \delta_0 + \delta_1 \ell nP_{t-1} + \delta_2(\ell nW_t - \ell nW_{t-1})$$
$$+ \delta_3(\ell nW_{t-1} - \ell nW_{t-2})$$
$$+ \delta_4(\ell nPF_t - \ell nPF_{t-1}) + u_{4t}. \qquad (5.2.5)$$

Glancing at equations (5.2.1) through (5.2.5), it is clear that anticipated values of variables play a key role. What kind of process generates expectations? Economists have not reached a consensus on this important question. Given this continuing controversy, it would be a mistake to prejudge the matter. Therefore, we estimate the equilibrium model under two different expectational assumptions that have appeared in the literature: adaptive expectations (e.g., L-R 1970) and rational expectations (e.g., Altonji 1982). Both mechanisms and their application to the equilibrium model are now discussed in turn.

Adaptive Expectations. Adaptive expectations means that expectations are revised on the basis of the most recent forecast error. Suppose that last year an individual predicted that her wage would increase by 6 percent this year, but this year's actual increase was 8 percent. If expectations are formed adaptively, her prediction for the next period will be revised upward by some fraction, ψ, of the 2 percent error. Algebraically, under adaptive expectations real wage expectations formed in period t, $(W_n/P)_t^*$, are governed by

$$\frac{(W_n/P)_t^*}{(W_n/P)_{t-1}^*} = \left[\frac{(W_{nt}/P_t)}{(W_n/P)_{t-1}^*}\right]^\psi. \tag{5.2.6}$$

Following L-R, we assume that the same adjustment coefficient, ψ, appears in the price expectations equation:

$$\frac{P_t^*}{P_{t-1}^*} = \left[\frac{P_t}{P_{t-1}^*}\right]^\psi. \tag{5.2.7}$$

Substituting equations (5.2.6) and (5.2.7) into the labor supply equation (5.2.2), and using the Koyck transformation equation (Maddala 1977, p. 360) yields

$$\begin{aligned}
\ell nL_t &= \psi\beta_0 + (\beta_1 - \beta_2\psi)\ell n(W_{nt}/P_t) - \beta_1(1-\psi)\ell n(W_{nt-1}/P_{t-1}) \\
&+ \beta_3(1-\psi)(\ell nP_t - \ell nP_{t-1}) + \beta_3 r_t - \beta_3(1-\psi)r_{t-1} \\
&+ \beta_4\ell nH_t - \beta_4(1-\psi)\,\ell nH_{t-1} \\
&+ \beta_5 UNION_t - \beta_5(1-\psi)UNION_{t-1} \\
&+ \beta_6\ell n(W_{nt-1}/P_{t-1}) - \beta_6(1-\psi)\ell n(W_{nt-2}/P_{t-2}) \\
&+ (1-\psi)\ell nL_{t-1} + (u_{2t} - (1-\psi)u_{2t-1}).
\end{aligned} \tag{5.2.8}$$

Similar substitutions into the unemployment equation (5.2.4) lead to

$$\begin{aligned}
U_t &= \psi g_0 - g_1\beta_1[\ell n(W_{nt}/P_t) - \ell n(W_{nt-1}/P_{t-1})] \\
&- g_1\beta_3(\ell nP_t - \ell nP_{t-1}) + g_2\Delta UNION_t \\
&- (1-\psi)g_2\Delta UNION_{t-1} - g_1\beta_6[\ell n(W_{nt-1}/P_{t-1}) \\
&- \ell n(W_{nt-2}/P_{t-2})] + (1-\psi)U_{t-1} + (u_{3t} - (1-\psi)u_{3t-1}).
\end{aligned} \tag{5.2.9}$$

In sum, the equilibrium system with adaptive expectations consists of equations (5.2.1), (5.2.8), (5.2.9) and (5.2.5).

Rational Expectations. According to the theory of rational expectations, individuals' expectations about the future are unbiased forecasts based on all the information available in the present. In the context of our problem, the most elegant method for implementing this theory is to specify models for all the exogenous variables in the system; solve for expected prices and real net wages as functions of these variables; substitute the relevant expressions for P_t^* and $(W_n/P)_t^*$ into the model; and estimate the entire system using maximum likelihood methods.

In the vast majority of cases investigators have rejected this approach because it is virtually intractable. Instead, a compromise method is employed. Define as X_t the variable whose expectation we wish to include in our model. The compromise procedure involves estimating an auxiliary forecasting model by regressing X_t on a number of predetermined variables, and defining X_t^* as the forecast generated by that model. Implementation of this procedure requires that several questions be addressed:

(i) What variables should be used in the auxiliary forecasting model? Altonji (1982) includes lagged values of X_t, and lagged values of other exogenous variables as well. A major problem with this approach is that it requires that forecasting equations for each exogenous variable be constructed. An alternative approach is to estimate a univariate autoregression, i.e., the equation for X_t includes only lagged values of X. The informational and computational burden of this approach is much lighter. In our case, preliminary experiments indicated that for both $\ell n(W_{nt}/P_t)$ and ℓnP_t, second order autoregressions generally produced very high R^2s. We therefore concluded that adding more variables would not contribute much to the explanatory power of the forecasting equations, and settled on second order autoregressions.

(ii) What sample period should be used to estimate the auxiliary models? One common practice is to estimate the equation for X_t using exactly the same sample as that used to estimate the model as a whole. (See, e.g., Pagan 1984.) Thus, if the basic model is estimated using data for 1929 to 1983, then the forecasting model is estimated over the same period. This approach has two striking implications: (a) people in 1929 base their forecasts for 1930 on a model estimated with data which come in part from the period 1931–1983; and (b) the processes that generate people's expectations in 1929 and 1983 are identical.

An alternative approach with less unpalatable implications is to employ a "rolling regression" method. Here a separate auxiliary equation for X_t is estimated each period, using only data available in year t. Thus, the structure generating expectations is allowed to change each year, and one never has to assume that people based their expectations on data that were unavailable to them. After some preliminary experimentation, we implemented a rolling regression procedure using 27 years worth of data. That is, the second order autoregressions used to generate forecasts in 1929 were estimated using data from 1902 to 1928; the forecast equations for 1930 were estimated using data from 1903 to 1929; etc.

(iii) How far into the future must forecasts be made? X_t^* is defined as the expectation of "future" X_t, but this begs the question of how many years into the future are relevant. If more than one year is relevant, what weights should be applied to the various years in order to form X_t^*? Altonji (1982, p. 819) reports that for prices and real wages, substantive outcomes are essentially unchanged when different reasonable assumptions are employed. We therefore choose one of the simplest procedures, to form X_t^* as $\frac{1}{2}(\hat{X}_{t+1} + \hat{X}_{t+2})$, where $\hat{X}_{t+i}$ is the i period ahead forecast generated by the auxiliary equation estimated for period t.

In summary, our implementation of rational expectations involves the following procedure: To form $\ell n(W_n/P)_t^*$ and ℓnP_t^* estimate

$$\ell n(W_{n\tau}/P_\tau) = a_{0t} + a_{1t}\ell n(W_{n\tau-1}/P_{\tau-1})$$
$$+ a_{2t}\ell n (W_{n\tau-2}/P_{\tau-2}) + u_{w\tau} \quad (5.2.10)$$

and

$$\ell n(P_\tau) = b_{0t} + b_{1t}\ell nP_{\tau-1} + b_{2t}\ell nP_{\tau-2} + u_{p\tau} \quad (5.2.11)$$

for $\tau = [(t- 27), (t - 26) , \ldots , (t - 1)]$, where $u_{w\tau}$ and $u_{p\tau}$ are random errors. This notation indicates that: (i) the parameter values depend on the year t in which the prediction is being made; and (ii) year t's parameters are estimated using data going backwards from year $(t - 1)$ to year $(t-27)$. Denote by $(\hat{\ })$ the estimated values of the parameters in (5.2.10) and (5.2.11). Now define $E\ell n(W_n/P)_{t+i}$ as the i period ahead forecast generated by the $\hat{a}$'s of (5.2.10), and $E\ell nP_{t+i}$ as the i period ahead forecast generated by the $\hat{b}$'s of equation (5.2.11). Then

$$\ell n(W_n/P)_t^* = \tfrac{1}{2} [E\ell n(W_n/P)_{t+1} + E\ell n(W_n/P)_{t+2}] \quad (5.2.12)$$

and

$$\ell nP_t^* = \tfrac{1}{2} [E\ell nP_{t+1} + E\ell nP_{t+2}]. \quad (5.2.13)$$

An Econometric Caveat.   Once the series for $\ell n(W_n/P)_t^*$ and ℓnP_t^* are computed, there is a tendency to think of them as "data" just like the other right hand side variables. Pagan (1984) and others have demonstrated that this is an error: because the expectations are generated by an auxiliary regression, they are subject to error, and this fact should be taken into account in estimation.

When the auxiliary equations are estimated using the *same sample* as the structural equations, it can be shown, in many cases, that failure to take into account the fact that the expectational variables are measured with error leads to their standard errors being biased downward—the expectational variables appear more "significant" than they really are. For such situations, formulas for obtaining correct errors have been obtained. (See Pagan 1984.) However, the statistical theory required to make such corrections in a "rolling regression" framework has not yet developed; the complexity of the problem may very well mean that a practical solution will be hard to find.

Where does this leave us? We think that the sensible approach is to continue to estimate models with expectational variables where theory indicates that it is appropriate to do so. However, the standard errors on the expectational variables must be regarded with special caution. Actually, this problem is less novel than it may first appear. After all, it is well known that a host of problems—errors in variables, omitted variables, incorrect assumptions on the error structure, etc.—may lead to biased standard errors. Applied econometricians should always present their results with some humility.

5.3 *Parameter Estimates*

In this section, we first discuss the results when the equilibrium model is estimated under the assumption of adaptive expectations, and then turn to the rational expectations version. In every case, all elements of the variance-covariance matrix of the error terms are estimated, because preliminary analysis indicated that the hypothesis that the off-diagonal terms are zero was rejected by the data.

The equilibrium models are estimated using the same data as the disequilibrium model; see appendix 4.1 for a description.

Adaptive Expectations. The adaptive expectations equilibrium model consists of equations (5.2.1), (5.2.8), (5.2.9) and (5.2.5). To begin, however, we estimated the system without the price equation (5.2.5), in order to make the results more directly comparable to L-R, who took price to be exogenous.

When we executed the numerical maximizing procedures described in chapter 3, the algorithm failed to converge. Moreover, some of the parameters appeared to be heading for absurd values. Generally, such behavior is a consequence of a very flat likelihood function. There simply is not enough information in the data to estimate all the parameters. This problem cannot be "solved," but one way to deal with it is to specify some parameters *a priori,* thus relieving part of the burden on the data. Rather than totally abandon the equilibrium model, we decided to follow this tack. Specifically, we chose to condition estimation on some value of g_1. What is a reasonable value for this parameter? Recall from equation (5.1.7) that g_1 shows the relationship between measured unemployment and unemployment due to intertemporal substitution. It seemed reasonable to assume that the two types of employment would move on a one-to-one basis; thus we set $g_1 = 1.0$. However, as noted below, we did some experiments with some other values as well.

The results are reported in the first column of table 5.1. The demand coefficients are of reasonable signs and magnitudes, more or less comparable to their counterparts in the disequilibrium model. The supply equation estimates are at least somewhat encouraging for the intertemporal substitution hypothesis: (a) positive values of β_1 and β_2 indicate that current hours of work increase with the current wage and

TABLE 5.1 *The Adaptive Expectations Model**

	(1)		(2)	
α_0	-0.975	(2.615)	-0.6090	(-3.368)
α_1	-0.773	(2.682)	-0.1371	(-2.996)
α_2	0.437	(8.006)	0.4089	(14.21)
α_3	0.00383	(2.775)	0.001315	(1.961)
α_4	-0.173	(-2.081)	-0.2587	(-5.834)
α_5	0.606	(3.442)	0.8081	(10.35)
β_0	-3.892	(-2.632)	4.696	(8.626)
β_1	1.005	(4.769)	1.232	(3.890)
β_2	2.862	(10.37)	1.486	(4.563)
β_3	-0.00232	(-0.808)	-0.001055	(-0.6094)
β_4	0.0754	(1.456)	-0.006552	(-0.2029)
β_5	-0.0561	(-3.434)	-0.05360	(-0.5719)
β_6	-0.0361	(-0.428)	0.03114	(0.1728)
g_0	-1.863	(-3.416)	-0.8720	(-2.870)
g_1	1.0	—	1.0	—
g_2	0.117	(1.363)	0.1085	(1.557)
δ_0	—	—	-0.08058	(-3.384)
δ_1	—	—	1.019	(184.4)
δ_2	—	—	1.015	(1.001)
δ_3	—	—	0.2552	(4.054)
δ_4	—	—	0.1642	(4.513)
ψ	-0.0119	(-15.01)	-0.03267	(-6.476)
ℓnL	497.5		652.9	

*Numbers in parentheses are t-statistics.

decrease with the expected future wage; and (b) the long run elasticity of labor supply with respect to the net wage, $\beta_1 - \beta_2 + \beta_6$, is -1.89, a figure which is considerably lower than most findings in the literature, but not outlandish. However, contrary to the intertemporal substitution hypothesis, the coefficient on the real interest rate, β_3, is negative, although it is statistically insignificant. It is also disturbing that the coefficient on the scale variable, β_4, is only 0.07.

But the real problem in column 1 is the estimate of ψ, which measures the extent to which the most recent forecasting error is used to modify current expectations. It is negative, and exceeds its standard error by a factor of 15. This makes no sense at all and implies that the adaptive expectations model is simply not a useful way to characterize the data.

The results in column 2 of table 5.1 show that the situation is not improved when we allow for endogenous price determination. A comparison of the loglikelihoods in columns 1 and 2 indicates that the price equation contributes significantly to the explanatory power of the equilibrium model. But the value of ψ is still negative and statistically significant. This result also obtained when the results were corrected for autocorrelation, and when several reasonable alternative values of g_1 were imposed. We are forced to reject the adaptive expectations model.

Rational Expectations. The rational expectations equilibrium model consists of equations (5.2.1) through (5.2.5) with $(W_n/P)_t^*$ and P_t^* defined by equations (5.2.12) and (5.2.13), respectively. Our first attempt to estimate the parameters met the same fate as the adaptive expectations model—there was insufficient information in the data to identify all the parameters. We again estimated conditional on $g_1 = 1.0$.

The results are presented in column 1 of table 5.2. The demand side results are sensible except for the negative coefficient on lagged labor (α_5), but it is statistically insignificant. The supply side results look quite promising for the intertemporal substitution hypothesis: β_1, β_2 and β_3 each have the expected positive signs; the long run labor supply elasticity, $\beta_1 - \beta_2 + \beta_6$ is 0.089, result which is consistent with much earlier work; and the coefficient on the scale variable, β_4, is 0.290, a figure which seems low but not absurd. The natural rate of unemployment, measured by g_0, is 0.0745, which seems quite reasonable. The coefficient g_2, which multiplies the change in the unionization rate in the unemployment equation, is positive but insignificant; this is not very different from the corresponding result in the disequilibrium model. Finally, as expected, the values of δ_1 through δ_4 are positive. A potentially disturbing result is that the coefficient on lagged price in the price equation, δ_1, exceeds one. This raises doubts about the stability of the model. Of course, to analyze the stability of a *system* requires that all the coefficients be studied jointly; we return to this issue later.

In contrast to the adaptive expectations results, we were sufficiently encouraged by the figures in column 1 that we decided to attempt some refinements. To begin, we re-estimated the system under the assump-

TABLE 5.2 *The Rational Expectations Model**

	(1)		(2)		(3)	
α_0	−1.928	(−3.280)	0.3406	(0.3020)	−1.200	(−2.300)
α_1	−0.758	(−8.251)	−0.8307	(−5.794)	−2.611	(−3.367)
α_2	0.561	(6.566)	0.1421	(1.108)	0.912	(2.955)
α_3	0.0121	(4.848)	0.02983	(6.276)	0.0437	(5.517)
α_4	0.100	(1.429)	0.1181	(1.421)	0.518	(3.045)
α_5	−0.159	(−1.222)	−0.2507	(−1.871)	−0.769	(3.658)
β_0	3.631	(5.620)	3.9803	(11.29)	4.240	(11.65)
β_1	0.122	(1.942)	0.01995	(0.9204)	0.0490	(1.483)
β_2	0.0803	(1.129)	−0.01823	(−0.5666)	−0.0283	(−1.011)
β_3	0.0231	(4.577)	0.01585	(3.648)	0.0157	(3.862)
β_4	0.290	(2.584)	0.2339	(4.666)	0.239	(4.978)
β_5	−0.232	(−1.081)	−0.2847	(−1.085)	−0.181	(−0.684)
β_6	0.0474	(1.235)	0.03405	(1.839)	0.101	(3.333)
g_0	0.0745	(10.06)	0.0544	(2.441)	0.0356	(1.080)
g_1	1.0	—	1.0	—	0.4	—
g_2	0.553	(1.809)	0.04770	(0.4962)	−0.0898	(−0.832)
δ_0	−0.0512	(−1.347)	−0.06340	(−0.8305)	0.0252	(0.340)
δ_1	1.013	(117.0)	1.023	(54.11)	1.036	(42.25)
δ_2	0.0556	(0.528)	−0.3970	(−1.413)	−5.842	(2.043)
δ_3	0.187	(2.281)	0.1694	(1.312)	2.501	(2.230)
δ_4	0.235	(4.846)	0.2820	(3.331)	1.549	(2.515)
ρ_1	—	—	0.8780	(18.38)	0.971	(33.01)
ρ_2	—	—	0.9225	(20.82)	0.866	(19.68)
ρ_3	—	—	0.9225	(27.98)	0.960	(40.22)
ρ_4	—	—	0.2388	(1.563)	−0.0738	(−0.762)
ℓnL	522.0	—	612.78	—	617.6	—

*Numbers in parentheses are t-statistics.

tion that the errors are autocorrelated. Specifically, define ρ_1, ρ_2, ρ_3 and ρ_4 as the first order autocorrelation coefficients in the demand, supply, unemployment and price equations, respectively. The estimated ρ's along with other coefficients are presented in column 2 of table 5.2.

Comparing the loglikelihood values for the models in columns 1 and 2, it is clear that the data reject the model with no autocorrelation since under the null hypothesis of no autocorrelation, −2 times the loglikelihood ratio has asymptotically χ^2 distribution with 4 degrees of freedom. A further interesting result is that the column 2 results are much less favorable to the intertemporal substitution hypothesis: β_1 is still positive but is estimated imprecisely; and β_2 is now negative, albeit with a t-statistic of only -0.5666. (Remember, however, the earlier caveat about the interpretation of the standard errors.)

Recall that the estimates in table 5.2 are conditioned upon $g = 1.0$. Perhaps the results would be more favorable to the equilibrium hypothesis under alternative values. We experimented with $g_1 = 0.8$, 0.6 and 0.4. In all cases, the results are qualitatively similar to those with $g_1 = 1.0$. For purposes of illustration, we record the values for $g_1 = 0.4$ in column 3 of table 5.2.

How do our findings on the equilibrium model square with earlier studies? Altonji (1982) also tested a rational expectations formulation of the L-R model and concluded: "The results do not support the intertemporal substitution model. For most specifications, the current real wage, the expected future wage, and the expected real rate of interest are either insignificantly related to unemployment and labour supply or have the wrong sign" (p. 784). Our results are broadly similar. β_1 has the "right" sign but is statistically insignificant; β_2 has the "wrong" insignificant sign; only β_3 has a "right" and significant sign. However, these results can be obtained only after g_1 is *forced* to have the "right" sign and magnitude. Based on the estimated parameters, then, the equilibrium model does not seem to be a good way of characterizing the data. We now turn to some other ways for evaluating the model.

5.4 *Other Results for the Rational Expectations Model*

Stability. The analysis of stability for the equilibrium model is somewhat less complicated than it was in the case of the disequilibrium model. We show in appendix 5.1 that stability requires that all roots of the following cubic equation in x have modulus less than one:

$$[(\alpha_1 - \beta_1) - \delta_2(\alpha_1 - \beta_1 + \beta_3)]x^3 + [-\delta_1(\alpha_1 - \beta_1) - \beta_6$$
$$- (\alpha_1 - \beta_1 + \beta_3)(\delta_3 - \delta_2) - \delta_2\beta_6]x^2 + [\beta_6\delta_1 - \beta_6(\delta_3 - \delta_2)$$
$$+ \delta_3(\alpha_1 - \beta_1 + \beta_3)]x + [\beta_6\delta_3] = 0.$$

Table 5.3 *R^2s for the Equilibrium Model*

$\ell n\ L_t$	$\ell n\ P_t$	$\ell n\ W_t$	U_t
0.9576	0.9977	0.9989	0.8628

Solving this equation with the parameters from column 2 in table 5.2, we find one real and one pair of complex conjugate roots given by x = 0.04988 ± 0.04795i and x = 1.0192. The complex roots produce highly damped behavior, but the real root exceeds unity and hence the system is not stable.

Our belief is that instability in a model should not necessarily be regarded as a fatal flaw. After all, some observers have suggested that the U.S. economy is prone to "inflationary spirals" when it is subjected to shocks, and instability may just be a manifestation of this phenomenon. Nevertheless, the finding is disturbing and creates some doubts about the usefulness of the model.

Goodness of Fit. For every year we computed the predicted value of each of the model's endogenous variable. When the predicted values are regressed on the actual values, the R^2s are as reported on table 5.3. Comparing these to the R^2s for the disequilibrium model (table 4.2), we see that there is not much difference. Both models do extremely well at tracking wages and prices, due at least in part to the high degree of serial correlation in these series. The R^2s for ℓnL and U are not quite as good as those in the disequilibrium model, but neither model is clearly superior along this dimension.

Phillips Curve. We follow the same strategy for finding the short run Phillips Curve for the equilibrium model as we did for the disequilibrium model: compute the values of $(\ell n\ W_{1982} - \ell n\ W_{1981})$ and U_{1982} associated with various values of real output (Q_{1982}), and fit a straight line to the figures so generated.[4] The result is $(\ell n\ W_{1982} - \ell n\ W_{1981}) = 3.774 - 49.99\ U_{1982}$. Recall that the disequilibrium model yielded the result $(\ell n\ W_{1982} - \ell n\ W_{1981}) = 0.1866 - 1.841\ U_{1982}$. Hence, the equilibrium model has a much steeper Phillips Curve—it is almost vertical at an unemployment rate of 7.5 percent. In this context, one should recall from the discussion surrounding equation (5.1.9) that the L-R model *constrains* the long

Table 5.4 *Phillips Curves With Alternative Unionization Rates*

Unionization rate	Intercept	Slope
0.268	3.782	−50.11
0.218	3.782	−50.10
0.168	3.774	−49.99
0.118	3.773	−49.98
0.068	3.771	−49.95

run Phillips Curve to be perfectly vertical. Apparently, given our parameter values, this tendency is manifested in the short run as well.

Recall that in the disequilibrium model, we took advantage of the fact that the Phillips Curve is derived by perturbing Q_t to estimate the relationship between the percentage change in output and the change in the unemployment rate. We repeated the same exercise for the equilibrium model, and discovered that changes in output have virtually no impact on U_t. In light of the result in the previous paragraph, this should come as no surprise. The equilibrium labor market quickly adjusts to perturbations to assure that U_t stays near its natural rate.

Unionization and the Phillips Curve. The parameters in column 2 of table 5.2 suggested that the unionization rate does not have a very important impact on the model's endogenous variables—β_5 and g_2 are both small relative to their standard errors. Simulations of the model under alternative unionization rates confirm this observation. For example, a massive change in the proportion of the labor force unionized—from 0.268 to 0.068—affects the measured unemployment rate only in the third significant figure. As in chapter 4, we also computed Phillips Curves under alternative assumptions on the unionization rate. The results are recorded in table 5.4. They suggest that the unionization rate does not have much impact on the trade-off between unemployment and the rate of nominal wage growth.

Marginal Tax Rates. Table 5.5 shows how certain key variables are affected by changes in the marginal tax rate. The responses are all very small. This is no surprise given that the coefficient on the net wage in the labor supply equation (β_1) is only 0.01995. (See column 2, table 5.2). Thus, for example, when the tax rate goes up, the supply

Table 5.5 *Impact of Changing the Marginal Tax Rate*

Marginal tax rate	$\hat{L}$	$\hat{U}$	$\%\Delta\hat{W}$	$\%\Delta\hat{P}$
0.143	5.231	0.0736	0.0372	0.0509
0.170	5.231	0.0737	0.0374	0.0509
0.204	5.231	0.0739	0.0375	0.0508
0.238	5.231	0.0741	0.0377	0.0507
0.271	5.230	0.0743	0.0379	0.0507

curve shifts up to the left, leading to less labor transacted and higher nominal wages. But because the supply curve is nearly vertical, the quantitative significance of the change is very small. Why does unemployment go up with increases in the marginal tax rate, even as labor supply is going down? This is a consequence of the specification of the unemployment function, equation (5.2.4). As the *current* net wage falls, workers choose unemployment because they expect their future net wage to be higher, *ceteris paribus*. Again, however, because β_1 is small (and g_1 is set equal to 1.0), the quantitative significance of this effect is low.

5.5. *Evaluating the Equilibrium Models*

The adaptive expectations version of the equilibrium model does not appear to be consistent with the data in the sense that it generates absurd estimates of the adaptive adjustment parameter. The rational expectations model does better in the sense that at least the coefficients with the "wrong sign" are measured imprecisely. Recall, however, that the only way to obtain these estimates was to *constrain* one of the model's coefficients to have a "reasonable" value. Otherwise, no estimates could be obtained at all. Moreover, the fact that the model is dynamically unstable is disturbing. On the positive side, the equilibrium model produces a good fit to the data in the sense of high R^2s between the actual and predicted values of the endogenous variables. But as we explained in chapter 4, this is to be expected in any macroeconomic model with variables which trend over time. We conclude that the equilibrium model has important deficiencies. In the next chapter we turn to a more careful comparison of the equilibrium and disequilibrium models.

Appendix 5.1

Dynamics in the Equilibrium Model

In this appendix we derive conditions for stability for the model (5.2.1)–(5.2.5). We begin by rewriting the deterministic version of the system using slightly different notation:

$$\ell n L_t = \alpha_1 \ell n W_t - \alpha_1 P_t + Z_{1t} \tag{A5.1.1}$$

$$\ell n L_t = \beta_1 \ell n W_t - (\beta_1 - \beta_3)\ell n P_t + \beta_6 \ell n W_{t-1}$$
$$- \beta_6 \ell n P_{t-1} + Z_{2t} \tag{A5.1.2}$$

$$U_t = - g_1 \beta_1 \ell n W_t - g_1 \beta_6 \ell n W_{t-1} + g_1 \beta_6 \ell n P_{t-1}$$
$$+ (g_1 \beta_1 - g_1 \beta_3)\ell n P_t + Z_{3t} \tag{A5.1.3}$$

$$\ell n P_t = \delta_1 \ell n P_{t-1} + \delta_2 \ell n W_t + (\delta_3 - \delta_2)\ell n W_{t-1}$$
$$- \delta_3 \ell n W_{t-2} + Z_{4t} \tag{A5.1.4}$$

where

$$Z_{1t} = \alpha_0 + \alpha_2 \ell n Q_t + \alpha_3 t + \alpha_4 \ell n Q_{t-1} + \alpha_5 \ell n L_{t-1}$$

$$Z_{2t} = \beta_0 + \beta_1 \ell n(1 - \theta_t) - \beta_2 \ell n(W_n/P)_t^* + \beta_3(r_t - \ell n\ P_t^*)$$
$$+ \beta_4 \ell n H_t + \beta_5 UNION_t + \beta_6 \ell n(1 - \theta_{t-1})$$

$$Z_{3t} = g_0 - g_1 \beta_1 \ell n(1 - \theta_t) + \beta_3 g_1 \ell n P_{t-1}^* + g_1 \beta_6 \ell n(W_n/P^*)_{t-1}$$
$$- g_1 \beta_6 \ell n(1 - \theta_{t-1}) + g_2 \Delta UNION_t$$

$$Z_{4t} = \delta_0 + \delta_4(\ell n PF_t - \ell n PF_{t-1}).$$

Viewing equations (A5.1.1) through (A5.1.4) as a system of difference equations, the key thing to note is the recursive structure: wages and prices feed into the equation that determines unemployment, but the reverse is not true. Hence, in investigating the system's stability, we need be concerned only with (A5.1.1), (A5.1.2), and (A5.1.4). Moreover, we can collapse (A5.1.1) and (A5.1.2) into the single equation

$$\alpha_1 \ell n W_t - \alpha_1 \ell n P_t + Z_{1t} = \beta_1 \ell n W_t - (\beta_1 - \beta_3)\ell n P_t$$
$$+ \beta_6 \ell n W_{t-1} - \beta_6 \ell n P_{t-1}$$
$$+ Z_{2t} \qquad\qquad (A5.1.5)$$

The characteristic matrix M of the system (A5.1.5) and (A5.1.4) has the following elements:

$$M_{11} = (\alpha_1 - \beta_1)E^2 - \beta_6 E$$

$$M_{12} = -(\alpha_1 - \beta_1 + \beta_3)E^2 + \beta_6 E$$

$$M_{21} = -\delta_2 E^2 - (\delta_3 - \delta_2)E + \delta_3$$

$$M_{22} = E^2 - \delta_1 E$$

where E is the forward operator.

Taking the determinant of M leads to a third degree characteristic equation: $Ax^3 + Bx^2 + Cx + D = 0$, where

$$A = (\alpha_1 - \beta_1) - \delta_2(\alpha_1 - \beta_1 + \beta_3)$$

$$B = -\delta_1(\alpha_1 - \beta_1) - \beta_6 - (\alpha_1 - \beta_1 + \beta_3)(\delta_3 - \delta_2) - \delta_2\beta_6$$

$$C = \beta_6\delta_1 - \beta_6(\delta_3 - \delta_2) + \delta_3(\alpha_1 - \beta_1 + \beta_3)$$

$$D = \beta_6\delta_3.$$

Substituting from column 2 of table 5.2 into the expressions for A, B, C, and D and solving the cubic equation leads to three roots: $0.04988 \pm 0.04795i$ and 1.0192. The presence of a real root greater than one implies that the model is unstable.

NOTES

[1]In some versions of their model, L-R include a wealth variable, but find that it has the "wrong" sign. Presumably, this is because that variable is endogenous. See Romer (1981).

[2]L-R normalize labor supply by a population variable that is corrected for changes in age and education. Implicitly, this constrains the coefficient on the scale variable to be one. In contrast, equation (5.1.2) allows the data to determine the coefficient on the scale variable.

[3]We also experimented with specifications including the level of unionization rather than its first difference, and no substantive changes occurred.

[4]As Lucas and Rapping point out, under the adaptive expectations hypothesis, the unemployment equation itself has a Phillips Curve interpretation.

6

Comparing the Models

We have estimated both disequilibrium and equilibrium models of the U.S. labor market over the period 1929–1983. The natural question to ask at this point is, "Which one is better?" We first discuss statistical methods for comparing the models, and then consider some nonstatistical criteria.

6.1 *Statistical Issues*

From a statistical point of view, comparing the equilibrium and disequilibrium model is far from straightforward. Generally, standard statistical techniques can be used to compare two models only when one of them is *nested* within the other, i.e., when one model imposes certain restrictions on the parameters of the other. Our models do not satisfy this requirement.

To get a sense of the problems involved, it is helpful to consider the following simple "generic" disequilibrium model:

$$Y_t^D = \alpha_1 P_t + \alpha_2 x_{1t} + \epsilon_{1t} \qquad (6.1.1a)$$

$$Y_t^S = \beta_1 P_t + \beta_2 x_{2t} + \epsilon_{2t} \qquad (6.1.1b)$$

$$Y_t = \min (Y_t^D, Y_t^S) \qquad (6.1.1c)$$

$$P_t - P_{t-1} = \gamma(Y_t^D - Y_t^S) + \epsilon_{3t}, \qquad (6.1.1d)$$

where Y_t is quantity demanded in period t; P_t is price; x_{1t} and x_{2t} are exogenous variables; and the ϵ's are random errors. Compare model (6.1.1) to the corresponding equilibrium model:

$$Y_t^D = \alpha_1' P_t + \alpha_2' x_{1t} + \mu_{1t} \qquad (6.1.2a)$$

$$Y_t^S = \beta_1' P_t + \beta_2' x_{2t} + \mu_{2t} \qquad (6.1.2b)$$

$$Y_t^S = Y_t^D. \qquad (6.1.2c)$$

The primes on the parameters of (6.1.2) indicate that the estimates of the equilibrium model are not expected to be identical to those of the disequilibrium model.

Model (6.1.1) is not, strictly speaking, nested in (6.1.1) because one cannot derive (6.1.2) simply by putting certain constraints on the parameters of (6.1.1). However, an *approximate* test can be designed by examining the value of $1/\gamma$ from (6.1.1d). If $1/\gamma$ differs significantly from zero, the equilibrium model would tend to be rejected (see Quandt 1978). Intuitively, under the equilibrium hypothesis, gaps between quantity demanded and quantity supplied are translated into ''very large'' price changes; this corresponds to a ''large'' value of γ and hence a ''small'' value of $1/\gamma$.

However, a glance at the disequilibrium and equilibrium models of chapters 4 and 5, respectively, indicates that even this approximate kind of test is not available to us. Of course, we could have constrained ourselves to the class of equilibrium models that was (approximately) nested in the disequilibrium model. But a ''good'' equilibrium model might have features that cannot conveniently be included in a disequilibrium model; to exclude such features would unfairly handicap the equilibrium model in any comparisons with the disequilibrium model.

The choice, in general, is between having fairly standard statistical methods for choosing between models, but needing to constrain one of the models to be not the best representative of the class, or having two models that are, in some sense, best in their categories, but having to do with less perfect statistical methods in the comparison. We opted for the latter procedure. For example, in the disequilibrium model it is computationally very hard to estimate off-diagonal terms of the variance-covariance matrix, so these were set equal to zero. Similarly, for computational reasons only two equations were allowed to have autocorrelated errors. But in the equilibrium model it is fairly routine both to estimate the off-diagonal terms and to allow all errors to be autocorrelated, and we did so. Presumably, this gave an ''advantage'' to the equilibrium model. On the other hand, in the equilibrium model, a separate equation for nominal wages would be redundant because the supply, demand, and price equations together determine the nominal wage. In the disequilibrium model, this is not the case, so we included a nominal wage equation. Here the ''advantage'' is for the disequilibrium model. One may also note that expectations are modeled explicitly in the equilibrium model—to the extent that this is important, the apparent advantage is again with the equilibrium model (although a skeptic might say that if we seriously misspecified the manner in which expectations are formed, we may actually have hurt the chances of the equilibrium model).

The benefit we hope to derive from this research strategy is that no one can complain that the comparison between the two models is rigged—we have attempted to give each one its best chance. But the cost is nontrivial, because we cannot take advantage of routine statistical methods for comparing them. We now discuss a heuristic method of comparing the predictions of the two models.

The Hoel Test. Pesaran and Deaton (1978) have argued that in comparing two nonnested models (hypotheses), their absolute "fit" to the data is irrelevant; what matters is the performance of each model when the other is taken to be the null hypothesis. When we compare hypotheses A and B, we are really interested in the question how well A performs relative to the data when B is assumed to be true (and, of course, conversely). Such a comparison is meaningful and compatible with both models "fitting" relatively poorly or exceedingly well. Thus, a model that fits very well in absolute terms could be knocked out of the saddle by the appearance of another model if the former does not perform well in the light of the assumption that the latter is true.

A reasonable heuristic test in the spirit of the Pesaran-Deaton suggestion is provided by a procedure introduced by Hoel (1947) for comparing the forecasting abilities of two models. In this procedure, the predictive ability of each model is examined not in isolation, but relative to the predictions of the other model.

More specifically, Hoel considers a single variable y for which predictions f_{0t}, f_{1t} are available from two hypotheses or models labeled 0 and 1 respectively.[1] Hoel's test is equivalent to estimating the regression

$$y_t - f_{0t} = \alpha + \beta(f_{0t} - f_{1t}) + u_t.$$

If α is nonsignificant and β is significantly positive, this is taken to be evidence in favor of H_0 against H_1, since it suggests that when the predictions of hypothesis 0 exceed those of hypothesis 1, reality exceeds the predictions of hypothesis 0. In short, the hypothesis 0 predictions are statistically closer to reality than the alternative.

In the present case we have four variables: L_t, W_t, P_t, U_t, which for symmetry of notation we denote as y_{1t}, y_{2t}, y_{3t}, y_{4t}. We denote the predictions of those variables from the equilibrium and disequilibrium models by the superscripts e and d, respectively. Thus when equilibrium is the null hypothesis, we have

$$y_{it} - y_{it}^e = \alpha_i + \beta_i(y_{it}^e - y_{it}^d) + u_{it} \qquad i = 1, \ldots, 4 \ (6.1.3)$$

and when disequilibrium is the null, we have

$$y_{it} - y_{it}^d = \alpha_i + \beta_i(y_{it}^d - y_{it}^e) + u_{it} \qquad i = 1, \ldots, 4. \ (6.1.4)$$

Equation systems (6.1.3) and (6.1.4) each represent a seemingly unrelated regression model (Zellner 1962). Denote the ith regression in (6.1.3) in abbreviated form as $Y_i = X_i\Phi_i + u_i$, where X_i is the T $\times$ 2 matrix containing a column of 1's and the column of observations on $y_{it}^e - y_{it}^d$, and where $\Phi' = (\alpha_i \ \beta_i)$. We can then stack the equations of (6.1.3) as

$$\begin{bmatrix} Y_1 \\ Y_2 \\ Y_3 \\ Y_4 \end{bmatrix} = \begin{bmatrix} X_1 & 0 & 0 & 0 \\ 0 & X_2 & 0 & 0 \\ 0 & 0 & X_3 & 0 \\ 0 & 0 & 0 & X_4 \end{bmatrix} \begin{bmatrix} \Phi_1 \\ \Phi_2 \\ \Phi_3 \\ \Phi_4 \end{bmatrix} + U$$

or

$$Y = X\Phi + U.$$

Generalized least squares estimates are provided by $\hat{\Phi} = (X' \Omega^{-1}X)^{-1}X'\Omega^{-1}Y$, where Ω is estimated from the sample variances and covariances of the OLS residuals of equation (6.1.3). Obviously, a similar GLS estimation can be performed when the roles of e and d are interchanged.

The resulting coefficients and t-values are displayed in table 6.1. Although the estimated α's are all insignificantly different from zero,

Table 6.1   Results of GLS Estimation of the Hoel Test*

| | Null Hypothesis is | | | |
	Disequilibrium		Equilibrium	
α_1	−0.000	(−0.15)	−0.000	(−0.01)
β_1	−0.275	(−2.90)	−0.722	(−7.73)
α_2	0.002	(0.48)	0.002	(0.48)
β_2	−0.323	(−3.93)	−0.687	(−8.49)
α_3	−0.000	(−0.11)	−0.000	(−0.13)
β_3	−0.378	(−4.05)	−0.602	(−6.62)
α_4	0.001	(0.42)	0.001	(0.43)
β_4	−0.497	(−4.32)	−0.500	(−4.36)

*t-values are in parentheses.

the estimated β's are all negative. Thus, neither hypothesis allows the other one to be rejected. We conclude that there is no appreciable difference in the forecasting abilities of the two models.

6.2 Other Criteria

Ability to forecast is not the only basis for comparing models. Other criteria must be brought to bear:

(i) *Plausibility of the underlying theory.*   As we noted in chapters 1 and 2, there are strong ideological overtones to the equilibrium *vs.* disequilibrium debate. Theoretical arguments that seem quite compelling to members of one camp have little appeal to members of another. However, the notion that an event like the Great Depression can be explained by intertemporal labor supply substitution seems incredible. In this context it is useful to recall that the disequilibrium model produces sensible estimates of excess demand each year (see table 4.3); implicitly, the equilibrium model sets excess demand equal to zero each year.

(ii) *Plausibility of the parameter estimates.*   It is rare for every parameter in a multi-equation econometric model to be "right" in the sense of having the expected magnitude and being estimated precisely. As the discussions in chapters 4 and 5 indicated, neither the disequilibrium nor the equilibrium model is an exception. Both models have some anomalous results. However, the main problem with the disequilibrium model—a scale parameter in the supply equation that seems implausibly low—pales in comparison to the problems in the equilibrium model: (a) the scale parameter in the supply equation is even lower than its counterpart in the disequilibrium model. (b) In the supply equation, the coefficient on the expected future wage has a negative sign. This rejects a key aspect of the theory underlying the model. (c) The parameter estimates taken together imply that the system is dynamically unstable.

6.3 *Conclusion*

Where does this leave us? The comparison of nonnested econometric models is not a straightforward matter; judging the relative merits of such models is partly a matter of tastes—some would even say of aesthetics. Hence, unambiguous answers cannot be obtained. Taking all factors into consideration, however, it seems to us that the disequilibrium model does a better job of characterizing the U.S. labor market than its equilibrium counterpart.

Having said this, we hasten to add that the disequilibrium model is relatively simple, and could be improved in a number of ways. For example, output in the model is predetermined; it would clearly be desirable to make it endogenous. (The same comment, of course, applies to the equilibrium model.) In addition, it would be useful to estimate a multimarket version of this model. This would allow exploration of the possibility that market clearing goes on at different rates in the union and nonunion sectors. The disequilibrium research agenda is rich and varied.

NOTES

[1]The heuristic aspects of the test as applied here derive from the fact that Hoel assumes f_{0t}, f_{1t} to be given to the investigator exogenously or to represent out-of-sample forecasts. If those conditions hold, the Hoel test is an exact result following from the Neyman-Pearson theory of best tests.

APPENDIX

Data

This appendix contains the data. The notation is the same as used in the text, and the definitions are listed in appendix 4.1.

Year	ℓnL	ℓnH	ℓnW	ℓnP	ℓnQ	Θ	UNION	U	ℓnPF
1929	4.785	119.710	−0.857	3.938	5.731	0.10	0.0	0.032	3.742
1930	4.736	114.000	−0.896	3.912	5.627	0.10	0.068	0.087	3.723
1931	4.676	107.290	−1.001	3.820	5.547	0.10	0.065	0.159	3.664
1932	4.589	98.440	−1.163	3.711	5.386	0.20	0.060	0.236	3.561
1933	4.586	98.090	−1.210	3.658	5.367	0.20	0.052	0.249	3.523
1934	4.577	97.260	−1.051	3.691	5.454	0.30	0.059	0.217	3.584
1935	4.620	101.470	−1.008	3.716	5.548	0.40	0.067	0.201	3.561
1936	4.677	107.470	−0.925	3.726	5.677	0.50	0.074	0.169	3.578
1937	4.726	112.830	−0.865	3.761	5.729	0.60	0.129	0.143	3.592
1938	4.662	105.890	−0.865	3.742	5.677	0.40	0.146	0.190	3.586
1939	4.703	110.320	−0.839	3.728	5.759	0.40	0.158	0.172	3.572
1940	4.739	114.290	−0.797	3.738	5.841	0.80	0.155	0.146	3.603
1941	4.805	122.180	−0.664	3.786	5.992	3.80	0.177	0.099	3.648
1942	4.864	129.510	−0.494	3.888	6.135	10.70	0.172	0.047	3.721
1943	4.893	133.310	−0.334	3.947	6.276	18.40	0.205	0.019	3.780
1944	4.888	132.700	−0.271	3.965	6.344	19.40	0.214	0.012	3.811
1945	4.850	127.730	−0.232	3.987	6.329	19.40	0.219	0.019	3.816
1946	4.859	128.950	−0.157	4.069	6.170	14.50	0.236	0.039	3.869
1947	4.880	131.610	−0.051	4.203	6.153	15.30	0.239	0.039	3.989
1948	4.809	122.640	0.114	4.278	6.194	12.10	0.231	0.038	4.138
1949	4.772	118.110	0.144	4.268	6.199	11.90	0.227	0.059	4.143
1950	4.803	121.870	0.204	4.278	6.282	13.10	0.223	0.053	4.171
1951	4.845	127.140	0.302	4.354	6.362	16.40	0.245	0.033	4.211
1952	4.853	128.100	0.367	4.376	6.398	18.10	0.242	0.030	4.225
1953	4.863	129.440	0.429	4.383	6.436	18.30	0.255	0.029	4.254
1954	4.827	124.870	0.461	4.388	6.423	15.90	0.254	0.055	4.257
1955	4.855	128.440	0.513	4.385	6.488	16.40	0.247	0.044	4.268
1956	4.872	130.640	0.580	4.399	6.510	16.70	0.252	0.041	4.301
1957	4.863	129.410	0.643	4.434	6.528	16.90	0.249	0.043	4.352
1958	4.832	125.400	0.681	4.461	6.523	16.70	0.242	0.068	4.339
1959	4.860	129.010	0.735	4.469	6.582	17.20	0.241	0.055	4.353
1960	4.869	130.190	0.781	4.485	6.603	17.20	0.236	0.055	4.333
1961	4.862	129.300	0.817	4.495	6.629	17.40	0.223	0.067	4.373
1962	4.883	132.060	0.865	4.506	6.685	17.70	0.226	0.055	4.374
1963	4.895	133.580	0.908	4.519	6.724	17.90	0.222	0.057	4.394
1964	4.911	135.830	0.961	4.532	6.776	15.60	0.222	0.052	4.371

Year	ℓnL	ℓnH	ℓnW	ℓnP	ℓnQ	Θ	UNION	U	ℓnPF
1965	4.943	140.240	1.006	4.549	6.834	14.80	0.224	0.045	4.392
1966	4.977	144.970	1.072	4.577	6.892	15.30	0.227	0.038	4.419
1967	4.985	146.240	1.132	4.605	6.919	15.70	0.227	0.038	4.450
1968	5.004	149.010	1.211	4.646	6.964	17.30	0.230	0.036	4.481
1969	5.029	152.810	1.285	4.699	6.992	18.10	0.226	0.035	4.503
1970	5.015	150.730	1.366	4.756	6.990	16.80	0.226	0.049	4.540
1971	5.016	150.770	1.431	4.798	7.023	16.40	0.221	0.059	4.600
1972	5.044	155.090	1.500	4.831	7.078	16.40	0.218	0.056	4.605
1973	5.082	161.150	1.575	4.891	7.135	17.00	0.218	0.049	4.743
1974	5.084	161.410	1.666	4.995	7.129	17.60	0.218	0.056	5.206
1975	5.055	156.790	1.756	5.083	7.118	17.80	0.207	0.085	5.286
1976	5.081	160.990	1.838	5.139	7.170	18.50	0.203	0.077	5.357
1977	5.116	166.650	1.911	5.201	7.224	18.70	0.198	0.071	5.479
1978	5.159	174.010	1.990	5.275	7.270	20.80	0.197	0.061	5.531
1979	5.190	179.520	2.077	5.382	7.302	19.00	0.186	0.058	5.831
1980	5.207	182.590	2.151	5.509	7.296	20.00	0.179	0.071	6.154
1981	5.216	184.220	2.239	5.607	7.321	19.90	0.176	0.076	6.349
1982	5.182	178.100	2.325	5.667	7.300	20.40	0.168	0.097	6.338
1983	5.199	181.160	2.349	5.698	7.336	18.90	0.159	0.096	6.275

References

Altonji, Joseph, G., "The Intertemporal Substitution Model of Labour Market Fluctuations: An Empirical Analysis," *Review of Economic Studies,* XLIX (1982), 783-824.

Artus, P., G. Laroque and G. Michel, "Estimation of a Quarterly Econometric Model with Quantity Rationing," International Seminar on Recent Developments in Microeconometric Modeling, Commissariat General du Plan and CEPREMAP, Paris, 1982.

Azariadis, Constantine C., "Implicit Contracts and Unemployment Equilibria," *Journal of Political Economy,* 83 (1975), 1183-1202.

Azariadis, Constantine C. and J.E. Stiglitz, "Implicit Contracts and Fixed-Price Equilibria," *Quarterly Journal of Economics,* XCVIII, Supplement (1983), 1-22.

Baily, M.N., "Wages and Employment Under Uncertain Demand," *Review of Economic Studies,* 41 (1974), 37-50.

Barro, Robert J. and H.I. Grossman, "A General Disequilibrium Model of Income and Employment," *American Economic Review,* 61 (1971), 82-93.

Barro, Robert J. and C. Sahasakul, "Measuring the Average Marginal Tax Rate from the Individual Income Tax," National Bureau of Economic Research, Working Paper No. 1060, January 1983.

Baumol, William J. and A.S. Blinder, *Economics-Principles and Policy,* third edition, New York: Harcourt Brace Jovanovich, 1985.

Bernanke, Ben S., "Employment, Hours and Earnings in the Depression: An Analysis of Eight Manufacturing Industries," Stanford Graduate School of Business, mimeo, 1984.

Blinder, Alan S., "Temporary Income Taxes and Consumer Spending," *Journal of Political Economy,* 89 (February 1981), 26-53.

Burkett, J.P., "Marginal and Conditional Probabilities of Excess Demand," *Economics Letters,* 8 (1981), 159-162.

Chow, Gregory C., "A Reformulation of Simultaneous Equation Models of Markets in Disequilibrium," Princeton University, mimeo, 1977.

Chow, Gregory C., *Econometrics,* New York: McGraw Hill Book Company, 1983.

Clotfelter, Charles, T., "Tax Cut Meets Bracket Creep: The Rise and Fall of Marginal Tax Rates, 1964-1984," *Public Finance Quarterly,* 12 (April 1984), 131-152.

Dickens, William T. and S.J. Lundberg, "Hours Restrictions and Labor Supply," National Bureau of Economic Research, Working Paper No. 1638, June 1985.

Eaton, J. and R.E. Quandt, "A Model of Rationing and Labor Supply: Theory and Estimation," *Economica*, 50 (1983), 221-234.

Fair, Ray C. and D.M. Jaffee, "Methods of Estimation for Markets in Disequilibrium," *Econometrica*, 40 (May 1972), 497-514.

Feldstein, Martin, "Specification of the Labour Input in the Aggregate Production Function," *Review of Economic Studies*, 34 (1967), 375-386.

Fisher, Franklin M., *The Identification Problem in Econometrics*, New York: McGraw Hill, 1966.

Gifford, Courtney D., *Directory of U.S. Labor Organizations*, 1982-1983 edition, Washington, DC: Bureau of National Affairs, 1982.

Goldfeld, Stephen M. and R.E. Quandt, *Nonlinear Methods in Econometrics*, Amsterdam: North-Holland, 1972.

Goldfeld, S.M. and R.E. Quandt, "Single Market Disequilibrium Models: Estimation and Testing," *The Economic Studies Quarterly*, XXXII (1981), 12-28.

Goldfeld, S.M., R.E. Quandt and H.F. Trotter, "Maximization by Quadratic Hill-Climbing," *Econometrica*, 34 (July 1966), 341-551.

Gordon, Robert J., "Price Inertia and Policy Ineffectiveness in the United States, 1890-1980," *Journal of Political Economy*, 90 (December 1982), 1087-1117.

Hajivassiliou, V.A., "Estimating and Testing an Aggregative Disequilibrium Model of the U.S. Labour Market," Massachusetts Institute of Technology, mimeo, April 1983.

Hall, S.G., S.G.D. Henry, A. Markandya and M. Pemberton, "The U.K. Labour Market: Expectations and Disequilibrium," University College, London, mimeo, November 1985.

Ham, J., "Estimation of a Labour Supply Model With Censoring Due to Unemployment and Underemployment," *Review of Economic Studies*, 49 (1982).

Hamermesh, Daniel S., "The Demand for Labor in the Long Run," National Bureau of Economic Research, Working Paper No. 1297, March 1984.

Hoel, P.G., "On the Choice of Forecasting Formulas," *Journal of The American Statistical Association*, 42 (1947), 605-611.

Laffont, J. J. and A. Monfort, "Disequilibrium Econometrics in Dynamic Models," *Journal of Econometrics*, 11 (1979), 353-361.

Lewis, H. Gregg, *Unionism and Relative Wages in the United States: An Empirical Inquiry*, Chicago: University of Chicago Press, 1963.

Lindbeck, Assar and D. Snower, "Explanations of Unemployment," *Oxford Review of Economic Policy,* 1 (1985), 34-59.

Lucas, R. and L. Rapping, "Real Wages, Employment and Inflation," in Edmund Phelps (ed.), *Microeconomic Foundations of Employment and Inflation Theory,* New York: W.W. Norton, 1970, 257-305.

McConnell, Campbell, *Economics: Principles, Problems, and Policies,* third edition, New York: McGraw Hill 1966.

Maddala, G.S., *Econometrics,* New York: McGraw Hill, 1977.

Maddala, G.S. and F.D. Nelson, "Maximum Likelihood Method for Models of Markets in Disequilibrium," *Econometrica,* 42 (1974), 1013-1030.

Malinvaud, E., *The Theory of Unemployment Reconsidered,* Oxford: Basil Blackwell, 1976.

Mankiw, N. Gregory, J. J. Rotemberg and L.H. Summers, " Intertemporal Substitution in Macroeconomics," National Bureau of Economic Research, Working Paper No. 898, June 1982.

Massourakis, N., F. Rezvani and T. Yamada, "Occupation, Race, Unemployment and Crime in a Dynamic System," National Bureau of Economic Research, Working Paper No. 1256, January 1984.

Modigliani, Franco, "Liquidity Preference and the Theory of Interest and Money," *Econometrica,* 12 (1944), 45-88.

Muellbauer, J., "Macromodels with Regime Changes: Discrete vs. Continuous Formulations of Non-Clearing Markets," Birkbeck College, mimeo, 1977.

Nadiri, M. Ishaq and S. Rosen, *A Disequilibrium Model of Demand for Factors of Production,* New York: Columbia University Press, 1973.

Pagan, Adrian, "Econometric Issues in the Analysis of Regressions with Generated Regressors," *International Economic Review,* 25 (February 1984), 221-247.

Pencavel, John H., "A Note on the Use of the Unemployment and Vacancy Statistics to Measure Some Effects of Government Legislation," Stanford University, mimeo, 1974.

Pencavel, John and C.E. Hartsog, "A Reconsideration of the Effects of Unionism on Relative Wages and Employment in the United States, 1920-1980," *Journal of Labor Economics,* 2 (1984), 193-232.

Pesaran, H. and A. Deaton, "Testing Non-Nested Nonlinear Regression Models," *Econometrica,* 46 (1978), 677-694.

Portes, R., R.E. Quandt, D. Winter and S. Yeo, "Macroeconomic Planning and Disequilibrium: Estimates for Poland, 1955-1980," *Econometrica,* 55 (1987), 19-42.

Quandt, Richard E., "Tests of the Equilibrium vs. Disequilibrium Hypothesis," *International Economic Review,* 19 (1978), 435-452.

Quandt, Richard E., "Econometric Disequilibrium Models," *Econometric Reviews,* 1 (1982), 1-63.

Quandt, Richard E., "Computational Methods and Problems" in *Handbook of Econometrics,* Vol. 1, Amsterdam: North-Holland, 1983, 699-759.

Quandt, Richard E., "A Note on Estimating Disequilibrium Models with Aggregation," *Empirical Economics,* 11 (1986), 223-242.

Quandt, Richard E. and H.S. Rosen, "Unemployment, Disequilibrium and the Short-Run Phillips Curve: An Econometric Approach," *Journal of Applied Econometrics,* 1 (1986), 235-253.

Rees, Albert, "The Phillips Curve as a Menu for Policy Choice," *Economica,* 37 (August 1970), 227-38.

Romer, David, "Rosen and Quandt's Disequilibrium Model of the Labor Market: A Revision," *Review of Economics and Statistics,* LXII (1981), 145-146.

Rosen, Harvey S. and Richard E. Quandt, "Estimation of a Disequilibrium Aggregate Labor Market," *The Review of Economics and Statistics,* LX (August 1978), 371-379

Salop, S.C., "A Model of the Natural Rate of Unemployment," *American Economic Review,* 69 (1979), 117-25.

Samuelson, Paul A., *Foundations of Economic Analysis,* New York: Atheneum, 1970.

Sarantis, N., "Employment, Labor Supply and Real Wages in Market Disequilibrium," *Journal of Macroeconomics,* 3 (1981), 335-354.

Smyth, David J., "Unemployment Insurance and Labor Supply and Demand: A Time Series Analysis for the United States," Wayne State University, mimeo, undated.

Yellen, Janet L., "Efficiency Wage Models of Unemployment," *American Economic Review—Papers and Proceedings,* 74 (May 1984), 200-205.

Zellner, A., "An Efficient Method of Estimating Seemingly Unrelated Regressions and Tests for Aggregation Bias," *Journal of the American Statistical Association,* 57 (1962), 348-368.

Index

Adaptive expectations: as assumption for Q-R equilibrium model, 71-73; evaluation of, 83; Q-R equilibrium model for, 76-78; *see also* Expectations; Rational expectations

Adaptive expectations equilibrium model: conclusions regarding, 77-78, 83; experiments with, 76-78

Algorithms: use of, in estimation, 34-36

Altonji, Joseph G., 3, 4, 71, 73, 74, 80

Artus, P., 6 n5

Auto-correlation, 41, 77

Azariadis, Constantine C., 14, 15

Baily, Martin N., 14

Barro, Robert J., 7, 10, 11, 62

Barro-Grossman (B-G) disequilibrium model. *See* B-G disequilibrium model

Baumol, William J., 9

Bernanke, Ben Shalom, 20, 42 n3

B-G disequilibrium model, 10-12

Blinder, Alan S., 6 n3, 9

Burkett, John P., 65 n6

Choice-theoretic foundations: use of, for analysis, 18-19

Chow, Gregory C., 7, 22, 27, 30

Clotfelter, Charles T., 62

Contracts, implicit: effect of, on wages, 15; incentive for, 14-15

Data: sources and construction of, for disequilibrium model, 44, 60-62

Davidon-Fletcher-Powell algorithm, 36

Deaton, A.S., 89

Demand, excess: estimates of, for unemployment predictions, 49

Dickens, William T., 7

Disequilibrium: definition of, 3, 6 n4, 7

Disequilibrium analysis: study of labor market for, 17-18; use of, to analyze unemployment, 4

Eaton, Jonathan, 21

Equations for Q-R disequilibrium model, 19-25

Equations for Q-R equilibrium model, 67-70

Equilibrium theory: use of, in labor market analysis, 3-4, 7-9

Error terms, 28-29, 32, 38, 41, 43, 44; *See also* Likelihood

Estimates, parameter: implications of, for public policy, 59-60; in Q-R disequilibrium model, 45-48; in Q-R equilibrium model, 74-78

Estimation: procedure for, in Q-R disequilibrium model, 44-47; in Q-R equilibrium model, 25-32; *See also* Likelihood

Expectations: role of, in Q-R disequilibrium model, 21; *See also* Adaptive expectations; Rational expectations

Fair, Ray C., 7

Feldstein, Martin S., 42 n3

Fisher, Franklin M., 44

Gifford, Courtney D., 61

Goldfeld, Stephen M., 36, 65 n5

Goodness of fit. *See* R^2 (multiple correlation coefficient)

Gordon, Robert J., 24

Grossman, Herschel I., 7, 10, 11

Hajivassiliou, Vassilis A., 20, 22

Hall, S.G., 21

Ham, J., 7

Hamermesh, 45

Hartsog, Catherine E., 2, 8

Hoel, Paul g., 89

Hoel test: for comparison of models' ability to forecast, 89-91, 94 n1

Income tax: effect of, on variables used in analysis, 58-59; estimate of effect of, on public policy, 58-59; *See also* Tax policy

IS-LM model: interpretation of, as disequilibrium analysis, 9

Jacobian, 36: rationale for, 36-38; use of, in disequilibrium model, 39, 41

Jaffee, Dwight M., 7

Koyck transformation equation, 72

Labor, observed quantity: estimate for, in Q-R equilibrium model, 68

Labor, observed quantity of: equation for, in Q-R disequilibrium model, 21-22

Labor demand: equation for, in Q-R equilibrium models, 67

Labor force, potential: definition of, for model, 60

Labor market: definition of, 7; equilibrium models for, 7-9, 67-86; rationale for study of, in disequilibrium models, 17-18; use of data for, in IS-LM analysis, 9; *See also* L-R equilibrium model

Labor markets, dual: analysis describing, 13-14

Labor supply: equation for, in Q-R equilibrium models, 67-68; as equation in Q-R disequilibrium model, 20-21

Laffont, 44

Laroque, G., 6 n5

Least squares, generalized, 88

Lewis, H. Gregg, 8

Likelihood estimates, maximum, 29-30; in Q-R equilibrium model, 28-30

Likelihood function: derivation of, for Q-R disequilibrium model, 33, 38-41

Likelihood ratio test, 77

Lindbeck, Assar C.E., 15

L-R equilibrium model: comparison with Q-R equilibrium model, 67-75; components of, 8-9; implications of, for

L-R equilibrium model (continued) public policy, 8-9; modifications of, for Q-R model, 67; and Phillips Curve, 81-82

Lucas, Robert J., 4, 8, 20, 25, 67, 71, 86 n4

Lucas-Rapping (L-R) equilibrium model. *See* L-R equilibriuim model

Lundberg, Shelly J., 7

Maddala, G.S., 32, 72

Malinvaud, Edmund, 7

Mankiw, N. Gregory, 4

Marginal productivity of labor: equation for, in Q-R equilibrium model, 19

Massourakis, N., 6 n2

McConnell, Campbell R., 21

Michel, G., 6 n5

Min condition, 30

Modigliani, Franco, 18, 42 n1

Monfort, A., 44

Muellbauer, John N., 22

Nadiri, M. Ishaq, 7

Nelson, Forrest D., 32

Newton's method: and variations of, 36

Okun's Law, 6 n1, 54

Optimization, numerical, 34-36

Pagan, Adrian, 73, 75

Pencavel, John H., 2, 8, 25

Pesaran, H., 89

Phillips curve: experiments with, 52-56, 58; in rational expectations equilibrium model, 81-82

Portes, Richard D., 49

Powell Conjugate Gradient algorithm, 36

Price: equation for, in Q-R equilibrium models, 70

Price adjustment: equation for, in Q-R disequilibrium model, 24

Price movements, historical: effect of, on nominal wage adjustment, 22-23

Prices: effect of income tax on, 59

Prices, rigid: in B-G disequilibrium model, 10-12
Probit models: relationship of, to disequilibrium models, 30-32
Public policy: implications for, 5-6; implications of B-G theory for, 12; implications of L-R theory for, 8-9

Q-R disequilibrium model: comparison with Q-R equilibrium model, 87-94; equations for, 19-25; formulation of, 17-42; implications of results for, 47-59; restatement of, 41-42; statement of, 38-41
Q-R equilibrium model, 67-86; comparison with Q-R disequilibrium model, 87-94; equations for, 26-27, 67-71
Quandt, Richard E., 6 n5, 20, 21, 22, 32, 33, 36, 42 n2, 42 n9, 44, 49,61, 64 n1, 65 n5, 88
Quandt-Rosen model. See Q-R disequilibrium model; Q-R equilibrium model
Quantity of labor. See Labor, observed quantity

Rapping, Leonard A., 4, 8, 20, 25, 67, 71, 86 n4
Rational expectations: as assumption for Q-R equilibrium model, 73-75; See also Adaptive expectations; Expectations
Rational expectations equilibrium model, 78-83; experiments with, 78-80
Rees, Albert, 4
Rolling regression, 72
Romer, David, 6 n5, 20, 85 n1
Rosen, Harvey S., 6 n5, 20, 42 n2, 61, 64 n1
Rosen, Sherwin, 7
R^2 (multiple correlation coefficient), 48-49, 61, 81

Sahasakul, Chaipat, 62
Salop, Steven C., 13, 14

Samuelson, Paul A., 19
Sarantis, N., 7
Simulation: in Q-R disequilibrium model, 49-52
Smyth, David J., 20
Snower, Dennis J., 15
Stability, 48, 62-63, 78, 79, 82, 83
Stiglitz, Joseph E., 15
Stochastic specification. See Estimation

Tax policy: relation to unemployment, 2; See also Income tax
Tax rate: changes in, and effect on variables, 82-83
Tobit models: relationship of, to disequilibrium models, 30-32
Trotter, H.F., 36

Unemployment: analysis of, in equilibrium or disequilibrium, 3-4; in analysis with rigid wages, 10-12; effect of, on public policy, 1-2; as variable in disequilibrium paradigm, 3-5; as variable in equilibrium models, 7-8
Unemployment rate: equation for, in Q-R equilibrium models, 68-70
Unemployment rate, natural: computation for, 63-64; relation of, to vacancy rates, 54-56
Unionization rate: effect of, on macroeconomic variables, 46; effect of, on Phillips curve, 58, 82; effect of, on supply of labor, 21; in L-R model, 9; in Q-R disequilibrium model, 57-58; relation to incidence of unemployment, 2; significance of, as variable, 23, 57-58; See also Wage adjustment, nominal
Utility/decision theory: See Choice-theoretic foundations

Vacancy rate: estimates for, 56-57; relation of, to natural unemployment rate, 54-56

Vacancy-unemployment relationship: equation for, in Q-R disequilibrium model, 24-25

Variables: construction of, for Q-R disequilibrium model, 60-62; definitions of, for disequilibrium model, 44; in disequilibrium model, 30-36; in equilibrium model, 30; as means to distinguish equilibrium and disequilibrium analysis, 30

Variables, expectational: standard errors in, 75

Variables, observed: in equilibrium analysis, 30

Variables, unobserved: in probit models, 30; in Q-R equilibrium model, 30; in tobit models, 30-32

Wage adjustment, nominal: equation for, in Q-R disequilibrium model, 22-24

Wage inflation: relation to unemployment, 1-2

Wage movements, historical: effect of, on nominal wage adjustment, 22-23

Wages, fixed, 4, 12-14, 15, 22-23, 24, 30; in B-G disequilibrium model, 10-12; efficiency of, in Yellen model, 12-13

Wages, nonmarket-clearing. *See* Wages, fixed

Wages, sticky. *See* Wages, fixed

Wage setting. *See* Contracts, implicit; Wages, fixed

Wages rigid. *See* Wages, fixed

Winter, D., 49

Yellen, Janet L., 12, 13

Yeo, S. 49

Zellner, Arnold, 90